NAVIGATING LIFE ANTHOLOGY

HEALTH, GRIEF & LOSS

CLAUDINE REID MBE

DIVINE Flow PUBLISHING

ISBN: 978-1-9196336-0-2

Layout and Publishing support Divine Flow Publishing Ltd, UK

Cover Design Marie Reid Chrispel Media, UK

Disclaimer:

This is a collection of stories by a diverse group of people. The views expressed are those held by each individual writer, and not necessarily those of Claudine Reid MBE or the other authors included in the collection.

PRAISE FOR NAVIGATING LIFE ANTHOLOGY

HEALTH, GRIEF & LOSS

"I've had the privilege of knowing Janet McNish before she became the much sought after Specialist Counsellor that she is. At that time she was a Creative Designer - interior and painting artist. Therefore, it's not surprising that in Knocked Down Before Lockdown her recollections read more like a novel as she paints a vivid picture of her experiences. Don't be fooled, each scenario unlocks an inspirational solution of how she used her own negative responses and attitudes to spur herself, and consequently the reader in how to be resolute and determined from within oneself, as well as, recognising the power of communication and connection to others.

Claudine Reid MBE has struck gold with precious stones as Janet McNish and her anthology colleagues give us truly practical and deeply powerful examples to see a path out of overcoming challenges, inspiring us to escape from the edge of personal disasters."

Juliet Fletcher
Founder Gospel Music Industry Alliance

"Faith is one of those women who radiates an inner peace that comes from God. This has been even more evident as she has walked through the pain of losing her mum. Faith's journey of grief is raw, honest and faith filled, and even though no two people experience grief in the same way, the gentle way she shares her thoughts and experiences will be a big help to anyone walking through their own grief journey. I am grateful to God that my dear friend, Sister and valued member of Jubilee Church has the opportunity to share her heartfelt testimony of God's faithfulness."

Pastor Kemi Koleoso
End of Life Care Educator

"Doreen's story made me feel hopeful. I could see through Doreen's personal experience that even when things may look bleak or hopeless, God is still in control. I was moved by the faith Doreen and her husband exercised, not to question God but to trust Him.

These stories are inspirational as they have been written by women just like me, so they are relatable.

Readers will be encouraged and they will have a book they can refer back to when they may need a word of encouragement. It would also serve as an ideal gift."

Doreen Black

"It was wonderful, very good content and style. I have never read anything on this subject before, so I found it very interesting from a personal prospective and that it was depicted in such a delightful and refreshing manner It will be interesting and insightful to all who will have the privilege of reading this work."

Lady Patterson

"I love the opening line's invitation to walk with Doreen through her intriguing journey to "unexpected blessing while navigating the course of her almost midlife!

This story is such an immense encouragement and testament of God's faithfulness and that He is never late. Thank you so much Doreen for blessing us with this heartwarming chapter of your life."

N White

"I celebrate with Doreen my sister in Christ and her dear husband about her miraculous pregnancy and safe birth of a baby girl. Doreen's concern for her husband and her being a liability reminds me of the story of Hannah and how her trust in God was rewarded.

Like Doreen, hopeful mothers must cry to God as Hannah did and as she did, ask for or accept prayers that God sends our way. My sisters in Christ if you want a miracle claim it, by faith and act, as Hannah did in 1 Samuel 1:18-19."

Lorna Jones

"Vulnerability is a word with which the church has a distant relationship. With this anthology, we have decided to look and examine Pandora's box of issues. It is essential in this time to deal with real issues, because people are looking for a real church. Yes! We know that Jesus completely saves, but do we have a Jesus who can deal with pain, heartache, depression and disappointment. Absolutely! This book gives a glance into a God who can deal with all types of life issues. The ladies who contributed to this book, shared themselves and will help others to know that the God we serve is a holistic God. He is concerned about all of our concerns, and can provide solutions and lessons that will enhance any life."

Andrea M Thomas
BS,MSEd, MSSSBL, G&T

"This book is detailing about different seasons in the lives of 13 Christian women who God carried through different seasons of their lives. I consider myself fortunate to know the story of some of the miracles that God has performed in the life of individuals. This did not prevent me been drawn closer to God as I read the different chapters. This book gives a clear understanding and the power of God in today's world that He still speak to His children and still works miracles in the life of individuals as He did in Bible days.

As in "FOOTPRINTS" you can see how God carried each writer into the next season of their lives. It's a must read for every Christian around the world. Like all works of art, no two books can be identical. But fear not: you have 13 powerful women of God purposely strengthening your walk, your faith and your purpose with God."

Minister Marcia Foster Norman

"I believed manifestations were essential for a fulfilling life, but realise spirituality is what was missing.

I finally feel equipped to address deep-seated family differences starting with my 17 year old daughter."

Paulette Lawson, Plantform Ltd

"Jose candid and sobering account of great expectations for life in a new country to the valley of becoming a widow in a strange land and navigating life with two young children. Her expansion on the gripping reality of grief, fear, despair and pain jumps off the pages, as does her faith in God as ...the defender of the widow and father of the fatherless... the God who never leave you and answers prayer. Jose's resilience reminds me that amid tragedy there is hope. This book provides wisdom and knowledge based on the lived experience of women we can all learn from.

Your circumstance is subject to change - believe in yourself. You can overcome and shape a better future for yourself be the blessing God has called you to be by enriching the lives of people in your sphere of influence."

Gloria Saffrey-Powell BEM

FOREWORD

Dear Reader,

I am writing to you like I am writing to myself.

As I turned the pages and began to read the gripping real life stories of 13 incredible women; the grit, strength and fortitude reminded me of my own life.

If I could turn back the clock, there are so many things I would say. I would start like this:

"What an extraordinary life you have ahead of you. If only they told us life would be like this. I would have a twin, (not a birth twin, but) a twin born of my mental instability. A twin who hinders me and often hates me but later, will save me from myself.

No one and nothing can prepare you for the things you will experience in life. For me it was the shame, the bullying and then the mental scars from the verbal and sexual abuse. It was the near fatal car accident, causing the loss of all my hair and over 250 scars on my face... then they wanted to amputate my shattered leg.

Sometimes, career paths choose you. I wanted to help people cover up the scars on their face, just like I did for myself. As the journey unfolded, I became one of the world's leading consultants in the beauty space!

A nervous breakdown at 47, followed by a series of fibroid operations, hysterectomy, hip replacement and open back surgery causing me to be paralysed for two years. All of this impacted my confidence, whilst I fought for my sanity. These life-markers have impacted my emotional and mental health, causing me to deal with grief and loss head on.

As you turn the pages of this anthology, may we learn, that the emotional expeditions are part of the journey. May we think about what we are able to achieve and the legacy of the life lessons.

"I am Stronger, I am Wiser, I am Better, much better"

are the famous words of Minister Marvin Sapp 2007 hit song - Never would have made it

Life has a way of making sense! These 13 stories demonstrate how courageous women have been able to turn losses into lessons, causing you to gain strength in the struggle.

I have learnt to speak those things that are not, as if there are - I currently have a Number 1 documentary which will trend on Netflix, depicting how I hated the skin that I lived in. It will be shot in Nigeria my second home, where my heart resides. Catapulted to the world stage with a successful career, I love the woman I have become; beautiful, intuitive, hardworking force of nature, continuing to inspire others. A global Citizen standing on the heritance of my parents.

Reader as you learn from these stories, remember, you must never give up hope.

From one ambassador of hope to another.

Eryca Freemantle

World leading makeup and beauty expert and educator

www.erycafreemantle.com

CONTENTS

INTRODUCTION

Life is a meandering Journey full of twists and turns, highs and lows.

> "You will face many defeats in life, but never let yourself be defeated" Maya Angelou

Sickness, Murder, Near Fatal Accident, Debt, Pain and Grief. In this book, 13 bold women uncover parts of their life journey. They delve into raw emotional and sensitive issues - from a life altering sickness, to the murder and loss of a child, to life after a near fatal car accident. These powerful stories share elements of the raw emotional pain, taking you on a journey of how, with fortitude, they were able to navigate a season in life when it felt like hope was gone.

The paradox is the muscle of resilience and strength is developed through the struggle, teaching us to a plethora of lessons whilst walking in the winter season and strain of the up-hill battle.

As you turn the pages of this Anthology analysing your own personal scars and remember that each scar is a reminder that you were stronger than what tried to take you out, each scar metaphorically says, "I survived".

The stories shared give hope and meaning to life - it serves as an encouragement to the reader, to let you know for every scar that was inflicted upon your life, you may have fallen - but you got back up, you are unique and as you stand in your individuality remind yourself, that you have already proven that you have what it takes to press on.

As you navigate life remember every season carries with it a new instruction, and every instruction requires something different from you. Stand in your strength!

My desire for every woman that reads this book is that she will see the beauty in the ashes of life, that she will find the strength to emerge more audacious, more determined and more empowered, thereby enabling others to increase their capacity for more.

To your progress

Claudine Reid MBE

1

IN SICKNESS AND IN HEALTH: NAVIGATING MULTIPLE SCLEROSIS (MS)

PAULETTE MORGAN

Shouldn't the world stop just for a second, or a moment even, to express its acknowledgement of this momentous, life-changing occurrence?

I stepped out of my front door on a crisp, clear, Spring-like February afternoon, appropriately dressed for the occasion in a calf-length black dress cut on a bias.

The elegant folds of my dress effectively minimised the pout of the small round 49-year-old belly I had developed from too many long days sitting at a computer and too few hours at the gym. Complementing my dress was a fetching black bolero, modestly covering my sleeveless arms and shoulders, small black clutch purse, black fascinator, and purple Office 5" heels fashionable enough for my 21-year-old daughter to proudly own a pair in black.

The birds sang in the trees, a light cooling wind blew, and children nearby played, laughing cheerfully with not a care in the world. Nothing stood still. It seemed disrespectful, somehow.

My two daughters and I climbed into the car, careful not to crease our lovely dresses. I settled behind the steering wheel, and we pulled away from the kerb for the ten-minute drive to the funeral service of my best friend and former business partner. Their father. My late husband.

Tony died on the evening of Friday, 25th January 2008. By a mere eight days later, on Saturday, 2nd February, we had pulled off nothing short of miraculous. Without hesitation, we unanimously decided that he would be buried in his beloved Jamaica, but first, there would be a celebration of his life in the UK with all our friends and family here. We set about with determination, undaunted by the fact that burying a loved one was a new experience for the three of us. We visited the local funeral home and ordered him a steel casket in silver, suitable for repatriation. Warned by a friend that their loved one had looked very ashy with death makeup on, we requested, *"Please, don't make him look ashy. We want him to look natural."* As the lady in the funeral home kindly solemnly swore to pass on our request, we were forced to suppress an inappropriate attack of the giggles. Our request for the service to be held the following Saturday was met with the response that it was improbable that a funeral director would be available at such short notice. Still, to our relief, one was located. By the time we left their offices armed with his measurements supplied by the morgue, the funeral and the repatriation flight the following Thursday were booked and paid for. The church had a function booked for later Saturday evening but could accommodate us for a 2 p.m. service. The caretaker was willing to work that day so we could hire the local school hall. Our church hospitality group took complete charge of preparations for the repast so we could focus on everything else. A cousin also visited and instructed me to just talk, and she would type. In a while, she said, *"All you need to do is edit, and the eulogy is done"*. I sent a photo of a smiling Tony to his brother, who designed and arranged for the printing of the funeral programme. And who visits wedding outfitters for burial clothes? We did! In life, he was always impeccably dressed. In death, there would be no difference. So we headed to the groom's department of a wedding clothing shop and purchased a silver-grey suit complemented by a cravat, a white shirt, and a pair of genuine Italian leather shoes.

I simultaneously made arrangements in Jamaica for a wake to be held on Friday night, then a second funeral service on Saturday, 9th February, in the church he had attended as a boy, followed by interment in the family plot. Four of us, including my brother-in-law, flew to Jamaica on Wednesday to complete the arrangements, and three dear friends followed a couple of days later.

So, on Saturday, 2nd February 2008, I pulled up outside the church and took the parking space near the bottom of the steps, next to the ominous-looking black hearse, gleaming brightly in the afternoon sun. I felt odd somehow, shaken. That single act instantly defined me as 'the widow', a realisation that had just then fully sunk in. I stifled the impulse to run and scream for more time to deal with the reality, but it was too late. This was it! I squared my shoulders, exited the car, and followed by my daughters. I placed one purple shoed foot on the bottom tread and walked purposefully up the steps to the door of the church.

Inside, the church was packed to overflow as family, friends, clients, and former colleagues gathered from across England to pay their last respects. The band played up a storm as the sound of 'How Great Thou Art' almost shook the rafters. There was an air of unspoken resolve to give him a terrific send-off, a true celebration of a life that had touched so many others. It was at this occasion that everyone discovered that Tony's first name was Harold.

We met at a Valentine's party the year we both turned 17. Purchased a flat at 21, married and moved to a terraced house at 24. By 28, we were first-time parents, business owners and moved to a detached house of our dreams. Expecting our second daughter at 33, we meticulously planned our future. We wanted a better work-life balance so I would take a back seat from our business and work in a supporting role when required, and I would only work outside the home if absolutely necessary.

We had been married nine years; our first daughter nearly six, and our second daughter was $4^{1/2}$ months old. That Sunday, Tony returned from net practice to say how badly he had performed because he had not been able to see the cricket ball until it had almost hit him several times. A visit to his optician reported an optical issue that should right itself. It grew worse. There followed consultations, brain scans, lumbar puncture, more scans, and consultations. Finally, after two years of stumbling in the dark, seeking an answer to this 'sight crisis', we received the diagnoses of Multiple Sclerosis (MS). Although unwelcome, the news brought some relief because finally, our uninvited 'guest' had a name. We had no idea of the implications, no clue of what would ensue. Ahead of us was 15 years of frustration, pain, and loss; yet, growth, revelation, and learning. There was very little official guidance available, so we learnt first-hand about the illness, as it impacted our world.

Multiple Sclerosis dominated our lives. The gradual but insistent isolation of illness became our reality. Over time, we were reduced from active socialising with friends and family to being stuck in the prison of our own home.

Contrary to our earlier careful planning, I now had to resume an active role in our business. Most of our clients were located within the same area, so we would drop the children off at nursery and school, then commute together by underground. One evening, while heading to the train station after work, Tony seemed to stumble; once, twice, three times. Each time, we had to wait for him to recover before moving on. To an onlooker, he must have appeared drunk. Our usual five-minute dash to the station became a halting fifteen-minute endurance test. He seemed fine afterwards, so we wrote the incident off as a one-off until one morning shortly after, we dropped the girls off and headed to the train station.

Within two to three minutes, our journey ground to a halt; his legs would not cooperate. He could just about stand; walking was out of the question. I left him waiting on the pavement and dashed back to fetch the car to take us back home. Work cancelled. Just like that, I had lost my business partner. I now had to take on the responsibility of running our business and home whilst being his primary carer.

To accommodate the loss of stability and facilitate his mobility, we installed handrails along the downstairs walls. These, plus the banister rails, enabled Tony to move around the house both upstairs and downstairs. He also had a pair of crutches, and a three-wheel mobility frame, and a ramp at the front door so he could take short walks in the front garden.

In the late 1990s, Tony was chosen to participate in the media campaign for the Multiple Sclerosis Society (UK). Travelling to the photo shoot, he was unable to control his bladder for the first time and wet himself—another downward turn. His natural sense of humour was ever-present. He related the incident to the cameraman that he had ticked off another symptom as it were.

Shortly thereafter, another relapse occurred that hospitalised him from April to June. The indoor handrails were now useless. By the time he returned home, I had converted our living room into his bedroom, complete with a hospital bed, hoist, commode, and an electric airflow mattress to prevent bedsores. By this time, I had completely taken over the business, and he remained at home, assisted by various carers. We installed a keyless entry system so he could let them in from his bed.

Having the carers was a godsend, but the invasion of our privacy was sometimes a nightmare. There was the incident where one went bursting in on our younger daughter as she was using the bathroom. The unreliability of agency carers who typically worked on weekends was another big problem. Often, Tony's bedtime long past, with no phone call to say they would be late or not arriving at all, I had no choice but to ask our older daughter to assist me in getting him into bed. Over time, our toned triceps would testify to the amount of hoisting and lifting that we had to do. Though not planned or deliberate, these shared activities caused our older daughter to feel like the third adult in the house and our younger daughter to feel totally excluded.

With little outside interaction, Tony became very knowledgeable of the TV schedule and would sit in his wheelchair, remote control in hand, flicking from show to show. Special cushions in his wheelchair kept him as comfortable as possible, but the progressive illness began to attack his torso so that if he tried easing himself into a more comfortable position, his body would flop forward, bent over in half from the waist up, and he would be unable to right himself. He needed extra upper body support.

There were no remissions; the illness was aggressive and progressive. We made constant adjustments to accommodate the relentless relapses. I decided to cease using agency staff and directly employed a carer on payroll instead. This new arrangement worked better because the new male carer and I worked as a team. I would leave daily schedules with specific instructions for feeding, medication, hydration, and the works.

Sunday was the carer's day off, but I continued to make it possible for him to attend church, after which I engaged in the very slow process of feeding him. Sitting still and waiting patiently as he slowly chewed, I would feel the strength literally drain out of my body. Unused to sitting passively, the full weight of my tiredness would bear down on me, and as soon he finished eating, I would dash upstairs to lie down as if my life depended on it. I could not eat a bite until I had rested.

Multiple Sclerosis worsened his sight and robbed him of the use of his legs. Two wheelchairs were necessary—an electric one for indoors and the lighter foldable manual one for going out. Another relapse resulted in him losing the use of his hands, and he could no longer safely operate the electric wheelchair, so the girls would use it to whizz around downstairs!

A major turning point arrived. The illness had finally robbed Tony of the ability to speak and swallow. Now, he had to be fed through a PEG tube attached to his stomach via his navel. I finally reconciled myself to handing him over to the care of a nursing home. With his care manager's assistance, we found one within a short distance from where we lived. Established in 1999, ironically the same year, he lost the use of his legs. His care manager later confided that it was something I should have done months before, but she knew it was a decision I had to make for myself. It was hard! But it was best for all of us. He had wanted to remain with the family, but he now needed round the clock care. Up to this point, the abnormal had become the normal, albeit a brutal one, as our lives had been controlled by his condition. With him gone and our schedules no longer determined by his needs, we had to construct a new normal. We had to rediscover ourselves. One consequence of the illness was that we had become like strangers in the same home. Each of us had devised our own survival routine, adapted to serve the needs of the man we cared so much about. In retrospect, we had to acknowledge that we had failed to do the best for ourselves in trying to do the best for him.

On returning from settling him in the care home, our home suddenly felt empty. And quiet. I immediately set about arranging the removal of twenty-one pieces of equipment. I returned the living room to its original use, but our family home had too many memories for us to bear, and we moved nearby into a modern apartment spread over one floor, with lifts where he visited us in his wheelchair once or twice.

I applied to voluntarily serve as a Justice of the Peace and was admitted to the position in February 2005. As a JP, I sat as a member of a 'Bench' of three in the local magistrates' court on Fridays.

Tony's condition worsened. Bedridden, he could no longer visit us. Christmas 2007 found him back in the hospital with pneumonia and MRSA. I had recently decided to move the girls back to a house where we could enjoy the simple pleasures of having a garden once again. One afternoon, between Christmas and the New Year, as we completed a house viewing and I got behind the wheel of my car, my mobile phone rang. It was McMillan's calling to ask me about Tony. There I was sitting, parked in Croydon street, having to discuss my husband's end of life care.

I was due in court on Friday, 25th January 2008, but on the 24th, I awoke feeling not quite right. I could not put my finger on what exactly was wrong, but I knew I was in no state to attend court the following day and duly asked to be excused. Friday came, and I felt no better, so I uncharacteristically decided to lie in for a while. Inside, I knew that this would be Tony's last weekend alive, and I planned to visit that afternoon and spend as much time as possible with him over the weekend, perhaps staying the night. He could no longer speak, so our conversations were monologues. Early evening, I entered his room and told him I was there. There was no acknowledgement. He lay propped up on pillows, hooked up to the oxygen feed with his eyes closed. I put on his favourite gospel CD and sat down in a comfy armchair in the corner across from his bed. Not long after, something made me move to the chair close to his bed, turn off the CD and started singing to him as I rubbed his head. Barely fifteen minutes later, his eyes popped open wide as he stared fixedly ahead. He was not looking at me! He breathed his last breath and was gone. I was alone with death, but I had no fear. I sat next to him, shocked at the suddenness of his passing from this life into another, but not terrified by it. I was amazed and unprepared since I perceived that he would most likely pass around Sunday, but here I was, dealing with the stark reality that it happened within such a short time following my arrival. My mind went blank. I tried to kickstart my brain. What happens now? What do I do? What is the next move? I finally got up, walked to find the nurse in charge, and beckoned for her to follow me. She entered the room and immediately recognised what had happened. Looking at her, I uttered my first sobbing words: *"Is that it?! My God, is that it?!"* She proceeded to switch off the oxygen feed, remove the oxygen mask, and lower the bed. There he lay for the first time in years, all traces of pain and suffering wiped from his face. He looked fresh as if he were taking a nap. The room felt enveloped in perfect peace.

The experience taught me some invaluable lessons that started me on my journey of becoming a Christian Relationship Coach. I learned more about marriage during the latter 15 years of illness than I did in the nine earlier years of health. I learned the gravity of the marriage vows and the commitment that is required. I learned the importance of friendship and communication in marriage. When intimacy was curtailed, friendship pulled us through and held us together to the end. Faith was also vital to endurance. Support from the family of faith helped build our resilience through those times we were so broken that we could not even pray for ourselves.

The experience had not put me off marriage, so I prayed and asked God for the opportunity to marry again. I asked Him for a man who loved me but loved Him more. I remarried ten years ago to a man who loves the Lord, loves me, and has enough room in his heart to be a true father to my two daughters. A man named Harold.

2

KNOCKED DOWN BEFORE LOCKDOWN: NAVIGATING THE UNEXPECTED

JANET MCNISH

An Unexpected Evening

I left the Osteopath's office full of hope after a practitioner assessment. She was able to help me achieve my goal of regaining my back strength and the elegance of my youth. I breathed in the damp January air of Southwark Bridge Road in London as I walked to the zebra crossing towards my car.

"Thank you, Lord, that was a divine appointment. Mariana can help me."

I felt respected and optimistic. Although she was much younger, she honoured my belief that a decline in health is not inevitable with age and that many diseases can be prevented or reversed with the right actions.

I waited at the zebra crossing for a driver at the opposite junction to indicate whether they were turning in my direction. When they did not signal or move, eventually, I decided it was safe to proceed. It was a big crossing on the main road, and they would be able to see me easily and stop in time. I started walking. They turned in my direction.

But they didn't stop!

BANG! The grey car hit my right hip and thrust me into the air. The depths of my belly expelled the deepest and loudest cry, *"Jesus! Jesus! Jesus!"*

My body was face-up, but I tried to reach my arms behind me to feel the ground. I saw that I was above a car in the air, flying horizontally, like in *The Matrix* movie.

BANG! The next thing I knew, I was lying on the road trying to get up, but I couldn't. I was on my back, trying to push myself up with my left hand, but there was no strength in my arm. I was shouting, *"You hit me on a crossing! You hit me on a zebra crossing!"*

Suddenly, a man came towards me and said, *"Your lungs are working perfectly well. Now, let's check the rest of you!"*

He was a paramedic. He asked my name. Suddenly, I was surrounded by lots of people in luminous jackets.

"We're going to have to cut through your clothing to attach the monitors. We don't want to move you..." I tried to protest, but no words came out.

I was drifting in and out of consciousness. This was one of my favourite outfits. It helped me to look and feel fabulous. I was taught to dress as I want to be addressed.

They started cutting my jeans from my ankles upwards, then my sparkly black quilted jacket and my cream silk jumper up the middle. Closely followed by people sticking patches on me and taking my blood, I was lying on the road in my bra and underwear. I felt the rough damp tarmac on my bare back—exposed!

I saw flashing blue lights. I heard the beeping of machines above the murmuring crowd that had gathered; my mouth was parched.

I started to panic as I was transported back to a past time when my clothes were being pulled away...and I had no power to stop it!

Terror rose in my throat; I couldn't scream. I froze! I tried to move but couldn't. Powerless! I could hardly breathe. I couldn't even cry out. I was confused. I just felt my clothes being pulled off as shame and terror overwhelmed me.

I heard a deep voice from my left, *"I've got you!"*

"Oh, my goodness! I've been watching too much *Empire*!" I was even thinking in American gangster slang.

Was that me? Was that God? Am I just reassuring myself? As a counsellor, I understood the importance of positive self-talk.

"I've got you!" This time from my right.

It *was* God! Immediately, I felt peace shine on me like shafts of light from Heaven through the dark sky. A profound peace beyond human understanding flooded into me like a river. I physically felt my whole body relax on the cold, damp tarmac as I surrendered to the paramedics' care. Although I was waning in and out of consciousness, I felt safe.

After a while, I heard the voice again: "*You know you need to forgive them, right?*"

I pretended I didn't hear. "*You know you need to forgive them!*"

God again! His voice was warm and tender yet challenging because I knew it was God's voice. The Creator of the heavens and the earth; my Creator and my loving Heavenly Father.

"*Already?*" I asked.

"*Yes, forgive.*"

"*Oh no, so soon? Can't I even have a go at them? Or call them names or anything?*"

"*Yes, now!*"

I hesitated. I did *not* want to forgive!

"*Lord, how can you expect me to forgive so soon? Forgiveness is a process. Twenty-four years as a specialist counsellor in trauma and relationships, you've equipped me to empower thousands of people to learn to forgive and overcome grave atrocities that they've experienced. You guided me through my journey of forgiveness. You've even helped me develop a*

Forgiveness Workshop. I understand forgiveness. So, do I really need pressure from you to forgive?" I silently protested.

"Well, you're going to forgive them anyway; you might as well do it now."

The voice was firm but kind.

I sighed. *"Okay...I forgive them and release them into your blessing!"*

Of course, I didn't mean it.

I felt God was very unreasonable. I've just been hit by a car on my way to help people transform their lives, with the possibility of potentially meeting my future husband as I was looking and feeling fabulous that day. The weighty silence felt very long. Hot tears trickled down the sides of my face and into my ears.

"Lord, I do forgive this person, and I do release them fully into your blessing."

I didn't feel any better, apart from knowing that I'd done the right thing.

God was right! (Surprise surprise!) I would have forgiven eventually. However, I didn't intend to do it sooner.

In the past, unforgiveness has robbed me of peace of mind and stifled my creativity. Unforgiveness hindered the relationship with me, others, and with God Himself. I've learned that the quality of our relationships determines the quality of our lives.

There are also health benefits to forgiveness. Harvard researchers proved that one five-minute episode of anger is so stressful that it can impair your immune system for over six hours. Forgiveness is healing.

In retrospection, I believe God did some healing in my body at that time.

I felt God's protection and assurance were still present in a different way from the rivers of peace. I had more of a heartfelt, knowing that my future was still bright. I rested under the protective *"shadow of the Almighty, The Lord... is my refuge and my fortress my God, in whom I trust."*

I think I was unconscious during this experience.

All this happened before I'd entered the ambulance.

"Do you want us to call your family for you?" The paramedics asked.

Having experienced many crises throughout my life, I have learned to calmly assess the situation, work out what was required, do what I could for myself, and request specific help from particular people.

My parents live overseas, and I have no siblings.

"No family to call."

"Are you sure? There must be someone?"

"No, it's fine; let just go."

"We think someone should meet you at the hospital," he insisted.

I sighed. Then I thought it would be good to see a friendly, familiar face; they called my friend Joanne.

They carried me into the ambulance and drove with blue lights flashing and sirens.

At King's College Hospital, the paramedics said to the Emergency Trauma Team:

"The patient was walking across a zebra crossing. She was struck by the vehicle. She landed on the bonnet. They travelled some distance, the car stopped, and the patient fell onto the road."

So, that was why I couldn't see the crossing when I was lying in the road attached to those machines.

"They travelled some distance! They travelled! As though we had agreed to go somewhere together. I did not agree to this!"

This meant the driver continued driving with me on their bonnet.

The next few hours were a flurry of X-rays, corridors, MRI scans, blood tests, drips, and beeping machines.

I was in a room by myself, connected to machines, and my door was a curtain.

I could hear the staff buzzing outside.

Around 2.30 a.m., I was admitted to Lister Ward, a trauma surgical unit and stayed for 17 nights. Injuries included spinal fractures, cracked ribs, internal spinal bleeding, vertigo, double vision and blurriness, widespread soft tissue damage, bruises, sprains, and Post-traumatic stress disorder (PTSD).

Days later, Pauline the Paramedic who managed an ambulance service in South London, visited her mother in our ward. When she heard my experience, she said, *"I don't want to sound like I'm minimising your injuries, but in my 27 years as a paramedic, I've never known anyone to survive such an accident and be so relatively intact. You could have died instantly or died soon after. Most survivors would be severely brain damaged, paralysed from the neck down, and requiring multiple surgeries with metal rods holding them together. Any or all of these would be normal for what you'd been through. Somebody is really looking out for you!"* She pointed to the sky.

I said, *"Yes, Jesus certainly is!"*

She looked at me like I was insane.

Whenever Pauline visited, she said, *"Janet, you're amazing, a walking miracle."*

I joked that I was a *sitting* miracle as I was unable to walk yet.

So, that was why the paramedics and medical specialists were so astonished and kept telling me that I was a very lucky lady.

Disability and Depression

I was relieved to be discharged from the hospital, sent home with a gutter frame weighted at the front and complicated to use. However, it was all I had as I was unable to stand upright by myself or bear weight on either leg. That evening, a carer came that had been by the NHS Rapid Response Community Team. I was to have four carer visits a day. Two one-hour physiotherapy sessions a week. I worked out how to get help with shopping, errands, and cleaning, etc. My recovery plan was coming together. The physiotherapist's approach was holistic and beneficial. She and her colleagues said I was their most determined patient, and they always felt uplifted and peaceful when visiting me.

Three weeks later, it was lockdown. COVID-19 pulled the plug on all non-emergency medical services, including my treatments and appointments. No one knew how long it would last.

I was left home alone with three visits daily from a carer. My friends were wonderful. They supported me in various ways, drove me to medical appointments, ran errands, cooked meals, regularly called for five or ten minutes, sometimes up to an hour, for mutual encouragement. We also laughed a lot. I felt so loved.

Although asking for help was difficult for me, I did not receive it as rejection if someone was unavailable. I respected their choices.

My plans allowed for these possibilities. SMARTER goals also helped.

I still had that deep peace within, despite the uncertainty in our world about the pandemic.

I was home alone, unable to walk or see properly and manage my care needs or cook a meal. I was still unable to lie down flat without triggering breathing difficulties which made me an emergency services patient several times. I'd slept very poorly since the accident due to pain and flashbacks.

One day in August, I said, *"My recovery is not dependent on the NHS and what Covid-19 is going to do. If it's to be, it is up to me!"* I sought advice, and a physiotherapist suggested I buy a rollator—a rolling walking frame with a seat.

I said, *"No way, my mother had one of those, and she's 85 years old!"*

I grumbled about that for a few days, did some research, then ordered a rollator. I was sad that my life had come to this. I was frustrated with the slow recovery and increased disability aids cluttering my home. Hopelessness was creeping up on me, but I caught it and took those thoughts captive. Eventually, I coached myself to reframe my predicament and viewed this as part of the journey to regain my independence.

One Sunday, I realised that I felt a sense of panic each time I heard cars drive past. So, I had to get out of the house—now!

I left with the rollator, determined to walk as far as possible, including crossing the side road. I was terrified because the last time I crossed the road, I was knocked down. I was still experiencing flashbacks. The fear was progressively gripping me, and I had to act against it. I was not about to get agoraphobia too.

A flashback is a vivid experience in which you relive some aspects of a traumatic event that feels like it was happening right now.

My main daily flashback involved me reliving the second just before the car hit me, over and over and over again!

As I started crossing the side road, a car came speeding towards me from my right. I panicked as he didn't stop but swerved around me.

Although I managed to get to the other side of the road, I was hysterical!

Thankfully, the carer arrived at my house. She could see me across the road and helped me to get back home. I was distressed for the rest of the day and unsettled for the rest of the week.

I recalled the first time I went out on the rollator with the physiotherapists. It took 45 minutes to walk the length of approximately two double-decker buses. I tried to practice several times a week despite flashbacks. Gradually, I managed to reduce my time from 45 minutes to 20 minutes.

I became more mobile at home, moving more comfortably by leaning on my glamourous walking stick and furniture surfing.

One day in October, I went to answer my front door, and I fell on my left hip.

I badly sprained my knee, ankle, and arm.

The ambulance crew persuaded me to go to the hospital. I was unable to stand on either of my feet due to pain. I've been in a wheelchair since, awaiting medical treatments delayed by Covid-19. I was discharged the following evening.

Other setbacks occurred: I broke my finger after stumbling on the Zimmer frame. Another week, I scalded 13% of my body as I was unable to hold the hot cup.

Three weeks later, hospital appointments had re-opened. I had 14 scheduled medical appointments in three weeks, across five different clinics and three hospitals. It was so exhausting. Depression and hopelessness taunted me. I doubted whether I had enough resources and strength to overcome this setback. But I could not afford to be depressed. I had to be laser-focused to fight for my recovery.

I was so tired of fighting. I wrestled with a loss of confidence. Self-rejection and thoughts such as:

"How long would I have to live my life in a wheelchair?

How could I rebuild my life?

Could I ever wear beautiful shoes again?

Would I ever have that healthy marriage?

Could I still love myself?

Could I ever believe I'm good enough?"

Most women have held themselves back from what they wanted in life because they fear they were not good enough. Not pretty enough. Not intelligent enough, not slim enough, not light enough, or not dark enough...

I feared being abandoned and that even my close friends would be tired of helping me, and I would eventually be cared for only by the Social Services. I was so fed up with this prolonged sickness. I assumed everyone else would be too. Therefore, I tried so hard to be an ideal patient. I minimised my pain and distress with my friends and clinicians, as I did not want to be a burden.

I wrestled with my own internalised oppression, in addition to microaggressions by others. I am now a statistic! A black British single, childless woman with visible disabilities in a wheelchair, unable to work or fully participate in society.

Who was I now? Did I truly believe that my intrinsic value came from my identity in Christ? That I was still God's chosen daughter loved unconditionally, endowed with many gifts and skills? Yes! I'd taught others how to manage their PTSD, thoughts, and emotions effectively. It was time to teach myself.

My ascent out of the well of depression began.

Lessons Learned

Fourteen months on, and although I'm more mobile than I was since that fall and the scalding accident in October, there is still no prognosis of when I'll be able to walk independently or drive again.

I had over 80 medical tests and only eight treatments due to Covid-19.

Nonetheless, I have chosen daily to live by faith in God, who knows my future and meets all my needs. I have also selected excellent specialist coaches for different areas of my life. In practical terms, I have implemented daily affirmations, healing scriptures, CBT, networking, journaling, and trauma techniques that have benefited my clients.

This was one of the most demanding battles I've fought in my life.

My resilience developed through previous difficulties, betrayal, fibroids, cancer, childlessness, a cancelled wedding, while other significant losses prepared me to cope.

Growing older, recovery feels more arduous. I've released myself from the "strong black woman" role in exchange for becoming an interdependent woman connecting with others in my vulnerability and abiding hope. My old and new friendships have become richer. I've learned to trust others more and to exercise courage to ask for what I need. I had to be specific and follow up, to be considerate of my friends' lifestyles, strengths, and limitations.

We live in unprecedented times. Everyone has their unique journey of navigating life.

This experience has been a journey of insecurity, pain, humility, courage, gratitude, and understanding myself and others more profoundly. Now, I am even more authentic and determined to overcome these temporary trials. I choose daily to learn to embrace abundant life.

How about you?

3

FROM DEBT TO FREEDOM: NAVIGATING FINANCIAL LITERACY

CHARMAINE DAWKINS-ALDER

Romans 13 v 8 (KJV): *Owe no man any thing, but to love one another: for he that loveth another hath fulfilled the law.*

My stomach is churning; my heart is pounding; my palms are sweating, and I held my breath. I find I'm singing again just above a whisper so no one can hear as I strain to say these words: '*The Lord is my strength and my song... and my song...Owe no man no debt, save love*'.

That was the verse we got from the Lord; so, why am I now standing in my kitchen doing all I can to stop myself from quaking and collapsing in a heap? I wanted to scream, but they would hear; the rest of the family were in the living room next to the kitchen. What would they say? The children would ask questions, and at that point, I could barely think, let alone answer any questions posed. And really, what was I going to say? I had to figure it out somehow.

How did we get here? How did this happen to me, to us? The letter and the phone call said if my husband and I did not pay the outstanding amount on the mortgage, the bailiffs would be coming the following day at 11 a.m. to repossess the house. The nausea was still there, but the quaking subsided enough for me to make dinner. My whole thinking was, *what can I do*? Where could I turn to stop this from happening? Through the fog of jumbled thoughts, I couldn't make any headway. Where would we go? What would happen to the children? What were we going to tell the family? What would we say to our friends and all the people we knew?

We ate in relative silence. I wanted to keep this dreadful news from the children for as long as possible, and the fact that my husband went into lockdown wasn't helping. Not a whisper came from him, and he just looked at me blankly when I asked him the way forward.

Perhaps you are thinking, why not ask our family? To be honest, although we were grown adults, like so many adults, talking about money didn't come easy. Going to family even in this desperate stage was not an option, as we knew neither family was in a position to help. I say 'knew', but with hindsight, I would say it was more than we assumed rather than asked.

When we finally went to bed that night, we did the only thing we knew how to do, and that was to pray.

My mind was racing for the longest time, and I got very little sleep. Morning finally came, and my husband arose and went to work. I had no strength to argue or question his actions, as incredulous as it looks now. He got up, washed, dressed, and went to work.

I hauled myself out of bed, got dressed, and went to wake my now heavily pregnant teenaged daughter. Then I poked my head into my sons' room and told him he had to get up and get dressed. By now, they knew something was going on, but they didn't ask. They just obeyed and did as I asked.

Anxiety now filled every cavity of my body; I couldn't sit down without my knees trembling uncontrollably.

The children finally settled in the living room in what seemed like an age. They sat, whispering and waiting for me to emerge from the kitchen. There was no grand entrance and no tears. I thought if I stayed calm, they wouldn't panic or grasp the gravity of the situation.

I don't remember the exact words I used, but I told them we were about to lose the house, and at that moment, I did not know what would happen, but I would try to do something. So, we prayed, and then I proceeded to make my list of calls to the only people who had an inkling of what was happening in our lives—my best friend and each of our Thursday prayer group members. I knew none of them was in a position to help us financially, but they would pray, and if push came to shove, they would do whatever they could to help.

I called the mortgage company as soon as I knew they were open and asked if they could give us a few days, but the person on the line calmly said there was no more time. They told me if the payment wasn't made by 11 a.m., the notice would be served, and the locks would be changed. Because the whole mess seemed so incredible and beyond what we ever imagined, we hadn't packed, not even an overnight bag. This meant we would be leaving with nothing.

A Wing And A Prayer

During a call, one of our prayer group members suggested we ring our Pastor. The thought had been sitting at the back of my mind, but again, like our family, I didn't want to go there even in this desperate situation. I didn't want to believe it had come to this; the fear of rejection and shame weighed heavily on me, but now I knew it was the only option.

I called the Pastor, and as I explained the situation, he was very understanding, and because of our brief conversation the day before, he had spoken to the trustees. I can't recollect the questions asked, just that he instructed me to meet him at the church office by 10 a.m.

Before leaving, I told the children we have prayed, so they were to hold fast and in no circumstances were they to open the door. I left home full of nerves as I made my way to the church office. I arrived a little before the 10 a.m. appointment. My mind was consumed with how little time there was left till we would be on the streets.

All I remember from the meeting was showing Pastor the letter and him praying for us. A few minutes later, the treasurer arrived and handed me a cheque, with which I headed to the bank. I was more than grateful we were halfway there. I now had the drive to the bank ahead of me.

At 10:30 a.m., I walked into the bank and went straight to the counter. I opened my mouth to talk, when unexpectedly, all the emotion I held onto overwhelmed me. I began sobbing, snorting, and shaking uncontrollably. I tried to assemble my words to explain to the cashier what was happening, but the more I tried to take control, the worse it got.

Thankfully, the cashier knew me and ushered me into the office, where she joined me a few seconds later. I still had no words; well, none that made any sense. So, I handed her the letter and the cheque. They had to get the money into my account and the mortgage company's account in less than 20 minutes. The cashier assured me she would do everything she could to get the money paid to the mortgage company by 11 a.m.

At 10:50 a.m., my daughter contacted me to say the bailiffs were across the road in their van. I repeated the instructions clearly and firmly, *'Do not open the door'*. I continued praying, and at 10.55 a.m., the cashier came back with a warm smile and said, '*It is done; payment has been made*'.

I called the mortgage company, my voice still weak and shaky, as I tried to comprehend what had just happened. I said payment had been made, and they need to inform the bailiffs.

I thanked the cashier again (making a mental note to get flowers and a card). As I gathered myself to leave, my legs were like jelly, but now, I could breathe a little easier. I then called my daughter to tell her the good news and that I would be home in a few minutes.

I sat in my car and let the morning events replay in my head; there really are no words to explain how I felt at that moment. I allowed the wave of gratitude, relief, and a multitude of other emotions to wash over me. The tears rolled down my cheeks as I gave thanks. I was so grateful to our church and for how God showed up and bought us through.

Becoming Financially Literate

I wish at this point I could say, end of story. The miracle-working God brought us through, and we never had to worry again. But you see, that was only part of the story. In the background, there were other debts, including credit card loans. Somehow, in a few short years, our lives had become a tangled mess of robbing Peter to pay Paul. The demands and the red letters were sadly a way of life. I dreaded seeing the postman because the brown envelopes kept coming. They never held good news, just another demand for payment.

Although we budgeted, what we had was never enough. We ended up in court again.

This time, the judge deemed that he could see payments had been made, albeit erratic amounts and on odd dates, so he gave us six months for things to regulate. Then, to my horror, he agreed to add the Mortgage company's fees for taking us to court to our already crippling outstanding debt.

It was now 2014, eight years had now passed since our crisis, and God bailed us out.

At this point, I had just been made redundant for a second time and was now trying to make a go of running my own business. Here, I was a registered company delivering Health and Safety and other related courses through a well-known awarding body.

We now had a regular income coming in, although not a large amount, but the mortgage payments and other bills were being paid, and Friday night takeaway was still happening. The red letters had stopped. On the surface, our lives looked okay, but the undercurrent of debt was sweeping me away. I was drowning.

I would often read and repeat Romans 13:8 and wonder, did we hear right? Or was I missing something? One minute I was holding to the word trusting God, and then another missed payment or an unexpected bill would present itself, and I would be gasping for air. The old story felt like it was stuck on repeat. The anxiety was no longer an occasional visitor but was taking up residency, and I knew I would not be able to hide it for much longer. Something had to change; the feeling of being wedged in a hole, unable to get out no matter which way I turned, filled my waking days. I was stuck.

There is a quote that says,

"Insanity is doing the same thing over and over again and expecting different results."

My family needed some different results; I didn't want to be stuck any more. I had to evict anxiety from the residence before it took over my life.

I remembered back in 2008, a friend had taken me to a forum called 'One Hand Can't Clap'. It was a vibrant and uplifting space where I met people who had been through similar journeys as me. Some had their own businesses; others had high profile jobs, all in this space. These people were up to something and going places. I always left on a high and with lots of ideas and possibilities, but I would get home, and life would take over.

November 2014 was a significant time in my life. Lorlett Hudson, the founder and leader of One Hand Can't Clap (OHCC), offered to coach me. I had declined because of the cost.

I found out the next forum was in a fortnight; I could not wait. I juggled the figures again, and the night before the meeting, I could hardly sleep like an excited kid going on a trip the next day.

I arrived just before the start of the meeting; the group was much smaller than it had been previously, but I recognize a few faces, and the buzz was still the same. I knew I was in the right place.

This was the start of my journey into coaching; everything worked well for the first few months, bills were paid, fees were met, and Friday night takeaway was still in place.

Then one month, I didn't get paid for some work I had done; everything came tumbling down like a pack of cards. My anxiety and self-doubt returned with a vengeance; my confidence packed up and fled so quickly I didn't know which way it had gone. I started questioning everything. '*What on earth had I been thinking, what was I doing? Who did I think I was? People like me don't have coaches. You know you can't afford this.*'

So, I tried to hide. I thought I wouldn't answer my coaches phone calls for a few days until I had the money to pay. I made up my mind to quit, and I would say so as soon as I felt brave enough to pick up the phone.

A few days later, I picked up the phone. It was not the conversation I was expecting. My sidestepping and hiding away were getting me nowhere. I realized the actions I was taking would keep me where I was and not move me forward.

Coaching is a process of looking beyond what I knew and enabling me to learn what I didn't know so I could grow. It is no magic wand but a growth process. I had to start showing up.

I was responsible for my actions; I had to show up and follow through on my word. The growth of my business was my responsibility. I had to ask myself why I struggled so much to look after what I created and enjoyed doing. To change my story meant having to leave our comfort zone to become comfortable with being uncomfortable, as no one else could do this for me.

Over the next five years, I learned to put structures in place and make plans for the year ahead. Spurred on by the coaching sessions, lots of prayers, honest and open sharing at the forum, helped me find the steps required to change our family's story. This is our hidden story of debt that, until now, I was too afraid to share. We are now just over two years debt-free. Business is going well, and now, we are currently looking to expand our client base.

4

LOSS OF MUM: NAVIGATING LEGACY

FAITH MATHANGANI

It was the 2nd June 2019, which will forever remain etched in my memory as it turned out to be the worst day of my life so far. The loss of my mum has not been an easy journey. She was my rock, the one I ran to when I needed a prayer partner, my encourager, my number one motivator, my friend, and my dear mother. As I leaned on her bed, my hand tightly clasped to hers. I saw her breathing slowing down and the graphs on the monitors taking a linear curve.

With tears streaming down my face, I watched my mum take her last breath as death stole her away from us.

This could not have happened at the worst time of my life, not saying there is a better time to go through bereavement; however, I was going through tremendous work pressures during this season.

One Saturday morning, my family and I were taking our football enthusiastic son to a match. We were all looking forward to it, then a few minutes before leaving the house, my husband slumped on the dining chair, looking very pale. He told me he was not feeling very well. He complained of a severe headache that seemed to have just come on and had numbness on the left side of his face.

After taking some pain killers, it did not seem to improve, and we decided to call 111 for advice. My husband and I were under a lot of pressure at work, dealing with tough issues that impacted his health. We had not realised how much the pressure at work affected us until this episode of illness occurred.

The ambulance was dispatched quite quickly but waiting for ten minutes when you are not sure what the next minute holds seemed an awfully long time to wait. I called my sister to help look after our children so I could follow the ambulance to the hospital.

On reaching the hospital, my husband was taken straight to a coronary care unit, which is a ward that specialises in the care of patients with various cardiac anomalies, as his blood pressure was extremely high, but his heart tracing was on the borderline of being normal.

They hooked him up on a lot of machines, took a lot of blood samples to run tests and at this moment, I felt so confused because of how fast it all seemed to have been moving. They took my husband in for head scans, and the doctors until that point had asked us a lot of questions but didn't give us any conclusive answers. We were asked to wait for the results of all the tests.

Later that day, they gave him a diagnosis that we were not prepared for. We knew they were trying to rule out many things, hence the various tests, but a mini-stroke was not what we thought we had to deal with.

He stayed in for a couple of days as they needed to monitor him closely. He was discharged after a few days but still needed to take further tests for a couple of weeks, following the discharge.

The Phone Call

While my family and I were still dealing with this difficult situation, I received a phone call, telling me my mum, who was thousands of miles away, was in an Intensive Care Unit.

When I received the phone call, I was driving to work. I remember screaming so loudly and crying to the Lord for help. All that was going on seemed so unbearable; my life was in a total crisis. My mum had taken ill several times due to an ongoing illness. She'd had various innovative cardiac surgeries and fully recovered, to the dismay of the doctors. This is because she was so strong-willed and a strong believer in God.

Previously, I never worried at those times when she fell ill because she turned around so quickly. However, this time, it felt different. Immediately, I booked a flight to go and see her the next day.

The flight felt like the longest eight hours of my life. On landing, I went straight to the hospital, and when I arrived, I found her in a stable condition. In fact, she was sitting on the bed, waiting to give me a big hug as she normally would each time I saw her. She didn't look seriously unwell to me at that time, or perhaps seeing me helped her to be strong.

After a week of being at the hospital, she was eventually discharged and went home, where she seemed to have been responding well to the treatment that was administered. This turned very quickly where again, after two days of being at home, her health deteriorated, and she had to go back to the hospital to have various investigations. My mum had always been strong and outlasted the medics estimation of when she should have passed away.

In 1996, when she was first diagnosed with idiopathic cardiomyopathy, a severely enlarged heart with unknown cause, she was given three years to live. She refused to accept that diagnosis and believed that she would live much longer. My mum defied the doctor's prediction and went on to live 23 years more than the doctor's calculations.

During one of the doctor's morning rounds, they called my brothers and me for a meeting to let us know that her condition was not looking good. Her heart was not working well, and we had run out of options for treatment. Although the doctors told us that we should not expect a good outcome, we still had a lot of hope. We kept on praying and believing that she would leave the hospital. I recall on Friday 31st May 2019, she was sitting on the bed and looked very beautiful. She told me that she has not looked as beautiful as she did that day in a very long time. She was glowing; her skin felt so soft, and she had a presence of peace that I could not put words to. On several occasions that day, she reminded us that she hoped to be discharged by Sunday that week, and we all just agreed with her that it would be possible. Normally, we'd wait for her to eat dinner, get her ready for bed, and pray with her before leaving the hospital, and it was not different on this day. We said our goodbyes and told her that we would see her in the morning, not knowing that this would be the last day she will talk to us.

The following day, we received a call from the hospital, telling us that we needed to come in immediately. I wondered why the rush, as she did not seem poorly the previous day and was even hoping to go home. I did not expect to see my mum in the state that she was in when I got to the hospital. She was unresponsive, occasionally moving her right arm slightly and was slipping into a coma. The doctors quickly called for another meeting to discuss the Do-Not-Resuscitate order. However, they asked us what we wanted to do, revealing that her kidneys had failed. Even dialysis would not have reversed the damage caused to her internal organs, whereby she has multiple organ failures.

We never left her bedside that Saturday; it was a dark day for us. I held her hands, prayed, cried, sang favourite songs, and recited Psalm 23, which was her favourite. It was a day filled with mixed emotions. I felt helpless, wishing that time would somehow slow down while at the same time, wanting the pain she was suffering to cease. My brothers walked in and out of the room, kissed her forehead, and kept telling her how we loved her. It was as if time stood still. I lost the awareness of everything that was going on around me. I cannot tell you whether it was sunny or raining outside.

On Sunday came the dreadful day when I had to watch her take her last breath. This was the worst life-changing day for me, which has been the most painful thing I have ever experienced. I could not help but think when on Friday, she kept insisting that she was going home on Sunday. She could have been referring to going home to be with the Lord.

To me, my mum was not only a mother, but she was also the only parent that I ever had because my dad died when she was pregnant with me. I have seen her walk through difficulties whilst keeping her head high. Bringing up three children on her own was not easy, but she did it, and she did a fantastic job. Her resilience to overcome adversities was admirable.

When my dad passed away, she was left with two children under the age of five and one on the way. She had no job and no husband to help her; it was devastating. Mum never remarried. She just concentrated on bringing up her children. She made sure we all went to good schools, never missed a meal, never lacked anything, and so losing her was losing a big part of my life. It left a void that I knew was impossible to fill.

On the day mum departed, I was numb for the first few minutes, followed by a feeling of a huge lump in my throat that made me gag. I felt quite nauseous and overcome by weakness that I could not stand. I had never known loss this close. In my years of working as a nurse, we learned about the stages of grief. I thought I knew it all until I went through the heart-wrenching loss of my loved one. My emotions were like being on a rollercoaster.

Believe it or not, even with a huge community of friends, relatives, and family around, I felt lonely. I was scared and gripped with fear. I was afraid of a lot of things that I felt had no closure. I was filled with tremendous sadness. I felt sorry for my mum and myself for different reasons. I looked for reasons and someone to blame. Sometimes, I felt the doctors did all they could then, and at other times, I found myself questioning her level of care and convincing myself it had been substandard.

The days following on after the burial, I was so exhausted mentally and physically.

Coming To Terms

As a family, we felt supported by our friends and the church community. They stepped in and gave pastoral support, practical help, helping with the chores, assisting with the funeral arrangements—all of which was needed, and we were grateful to God that He made that possible. This is where I saw the verse Psalm 46:10 come alive in my life. *Our Lord is our present help in times of trouble*. God worked through the lives of so many people to bring comfort and just love on us when we needed to feel God's love the most. Amid this, we still found people who, without intending to say the wrong things and simply wanting to help us understand or overcome the grief, would say all the wrong things such as.

'It is God's will that she has gone.'

'It's God's timing.'

'She is resting in peace and she has no more pain.'

'It's her rapture.'

'It is well'.

Well, it did not feel like it was for me. All I knew was my only parent, who I spoke to every day, was no longer here. While what they said could have had some degree of truth at that moment, it was better left unsaid. At that moment, most of those words were no comfort and only made me feel lower.

The most difficult time was when I returned to the UK. I used to call my mum every morning after the school run. I remember reaching for the phone a couple of times to call and remembered she was no longer there. I felt so frustrated. I missed calling her terribly.

God's grace gave me the strength to help me realise and accept mum was not coming back. It also helped me develop positive habits to change the negative emotions associated with the great loss of my mum, including all the negative experiences I have encountered in the past two years.

Life is unpredictable. We all experience pain in life, and just like no two waves are the same, I have realised that every loss is different for everyone, and we experience brokenness in different ways.

The pain we experience points to God's story. He turns all our negative experiences into stories that glorify Him. My mum always reminded me to remove my focus from things I had no control over. This seemed like a good reminder to draw strength from.

Legacy

Looking back, even though the events of 2019 were challenging, I can see the hand of God in every situation. I know the Lord placed me in an advantageous position to deal with all the pain.

In life, the nature of battles varies for everyone; however, the key to winning is to rely on the Lord and trust Him completely.

I am tremendously blessed for being in a church that has enabled me to be part of a small group that meets every week, and I have brothers and sisters who are incredibly supportive in all areas of my life. This group is vital to me because it is not only where I get help but also where I share my experiences to encourage other people.

This type of encouraging environment helps us to be a blessing to one another and do life together. My church family were always there for me when I went through challenges and helped me to see the light again.

The word of God was my anchor during this season of grief and illness. I spent a lot of time reading the Bible. I listened to uplifting Christian worship songs, which was a great source of strength. Worshipping God made me shift my focus off my situations and onto Him. When I magnify the Lord, my perspective changed, and I found my moods changed for the better.

The Bible tells us that life and death are in the power of our tongue. I decided to watch the words and thoughts that I entertained, as I would naturally gravitate towards negative thoughts and words. However, I knew the Holy Spirit would enable me to change my situation by changing my thoughts and my words. By doing this, God gave me supernatural peace as I continued to trust in Him for heavenly support.

Focusing on the people who expect me to show up daily by being strong, such as my husband and my two boys, gave me the strength to get up when life was knocking me down. This is my daily motivation, and digging deep daily to find my silver lining became even more important for me. Each time I am enveloped with sadness or tempted to have a pity party, I think of the moments I could be missing out on spending time with my children and husband. This usually helps me spring back up and live in the moment. I owe them a strong mother and wife, so each time I do not deliver that to them, it not only affects me but impacts my immediate family and the circles of people around me.

I also decided to set a firm rule to be focused on continuing the legacy my mum left. My mum lived a generous life. She was a giver in the community and always involved in Church.

In that same spirit of generosity, I am now actively involved in running an organisation that helps the less privileged children, which is what my mum loved doing. In this way, her presence is being felt, as the things she used to do, I am now continuing. I get a lot of comfort, knowing that my mum's loss is not the end of her story, and I will see her again one day. This work will be here for generations to come, and mum is still being a blessing to the kingdom of God.

5

UNEXPECTED BLESSINGS: NAVIGATING THE COURSE OF LIFE

DOREEN DOUGLAS

Life has a way of throwing the unexpected at us. Why me, you may ask? Why not is my reply? Sit back and travel with me as I open my life and share how I navigated (what?) against all odds at this juncture of my life.

Many of us dream of getting married, having children, and living a life of bliss, particularly when we wait for many years. I was no different.

I want you to know that nothing is impossible with God as He specialises in the things that appear impossible. You and I are important to God, and He longs to grant us the desires of our heart, even when others disbelieve based on life's observations. Please, realise that it is okay to wonder or think, '*What if?*' However, it's never okay to distrust God by thinking that we receive more than is bearable. My story may resonate with many women. We will, therefore, laugh and cry together. Let me kindly hold your hand, and let's walk through this journey together.

In February 2004, I was due to undergo a myomectomy, having been informed in 2003 that I had four fibroids. I felt devastated initially, given the things that I had heard, such as one cannot have a baby when you have fibroids. I was told that I had to remove them. With much deliberation and prayer, I decided to postpone surgery until my husband and I completed Bible school in the United States from August 2003 until June 2005. I guess I decided to put God's work first before my own needs.

Reflecting, I have no idea why I decided to do that. My husband left the decision totally up to me, and I did not feel any pressure from the rest of the family to undertake the surgery. It was not until April 2006 that an Obstetrics/Gynaecology consultant informed me that one of the fibroids was nearly as large as a grapefruit. Can you imagine how I felt? I thought I should have undertaken surgery in 2004, and maybe they would not have increased in size, had I put myself first? I began to question my judgement and query God's plan. Had I made the wrong decision? I was almost hyperventilating while leaving the hospital, out of sheer worry about my prospects of conceiving at my age. I heard that fibroids are prevalent in the Afro-Caribbean community. In the absence of statistical evidence, I could not support this claim.

In 2006, on our return to the United Kingdom, I was placed on the waiting list, and I eagerly awaited a date for surgery within six months. I felt as if I was waiting for an eternity, despite occupying myself to prevent worry. I became involved in as many activities as possible in church and work. In March 2007, I successfully underwent surgery, and due to a speedy recovery, I was able to return to work within nine weeks of the recommended twelve. I was generally fit and healthy before my knowledge of discovering fibroids. Life carried on in the usual manner, with the exception that my body felt cleansed and fertile. Words cannot express how I felt. It was a sensation of the gift of a new lease of life and was eager for exploration.

After surgery in 2007, the consultant suggested that we attend an IVF consultancy appointment, which we attended to understand the process better. The consultant told us that due to my age, an anonymous donor was recommended as they could not use my eggs; however, they could use my husband's sperm as he was much younger by six years, and therefore, this was advisable. My husband and I stared at each other throughout the consultation and thought, ethically and from our Christian perspective, we could not consent to this option under any condition. We, therefore, thanked the consultant politely and told him that *"if the Lord wants us to have a baby, it will have to be a miracle from God, but IVF is not for us."* The consultant looked at us as if we were totally from another planet as the medical prognoses were not in our favour. They, however, respected our faith and final decision. We were warned that this would be the only opportunity to start a family, and that time was not in my favour. I calculated that basically, I had missed the biological clock by maybe eight years. I was not even entitled to free IVF, as the cut-off limit was 35. We decided to explore fostering.

I felt as if I had let my husband down. He should have married a younger woman within a childbearing age band, which would have prevented this scenario. My hubby reassured me, exclaiming, *"What will be will be"*, comforting me and conveying that God knew best. He respectfully remarked, *"If it is God's will, we will have a child and if not, then we must come to terms with our situation."* His calmness externally was appreciated; nevertheless, only he knew the impact. He was young with the expectations of having a family of his own. He left the West Indies, and for what, a woman that appears unable to produce him a child? This was my belief, possibly what he may have thought as he never shared such deep intimate thoughts or emotions. I guess he was trying to protect me by softening the despondence. For a short period, I thought that he should find Hagar in the Bible, *'maybe I should allow IVF, especially as his body was intact'*. I quickly pulled my thoughts and emotions together and asked God for peace of mind and assurance that we were doing the right thing. At the back of my mind was a nagging feeling, *'You can still try; it's not wrong.'* God would not punish us if we tried IVF at least once. After all, God allowed medical science to develop such treatment for couples/women like me. I was clearly trying to justify my rationale in favour of IVF. I decided to silence those voices racing through my mind almost daily. I thanked God for all the wonderful things that I already had accomplished: a fulfilling career, a great family, and a good husband despite our differences, cultural expectations/lifestyles, and upbringing.

God's Intended Deed

In January 2009, I distinctively recalled being at church. It was Missions Sunday, and we were moderating the service. I asked Pastor if I could pray for him. On his warm reply, I gently laid my hands on his shoulder and prayed quietly. I proceeded downstairs to obtain a drink of water, and a sister (now a pastor) approached me. She requested if she could pray for me at the leading of the Holy Spirit. I openly accepted, and she prayed discretely but with fervour. I smiled in acceptance before fetching the water from the kitchen.

June/July 2009 are significant periods of my life in this journey, as you will discover. I recall feeling unwell at work and also at home. My joints ached; my breasts appeared to have swollen; my sense of taste and smell was different, but I could not detect exactly what was going on in my body. I wondered if I was seriously ill. I appeared fit and healthy much of my life; therefore, this sudden change was alarming. I mentioned the symptoms to my husband, and we agreed to arrange an appointment with the GP to explore my concerns.

On entering the GP's room, sitting down quickly, I began to share such issues as mentioned above and asked if I could take a pregnancy test. He looked at me sympathetically, as if to think, you are in your late 40s; the probability may appear unlikely. He proceeded to encourage me to purchase a pregnancy kit from the local Pharmacy.

I actually thought that the test could be administered at that appointment. The GP informed me that such tests are no longer done at the surgery.

I called my husband and conveyed my experience and said, *"I am going to purchase a pregnancy kit on my way home"*. I was so afraid to actually ask for it; my emotions at this point were telling me that I would be judged again due to my age. Maybe the assistant would think that it was for my daughter, but not for me. I purchased the kit and hid it in the bottom of my bag. I must have read it several times, checking that I fully understood the instructions. Please, realise that this world was alien to me, and it was the world of just us two and no more.

I finally picked up the courage to take the test. My hands were hot and sticky; my heart was pumping excessively as if I could hear the sound of thunder. Sweat was dripping down my face as the wait appeared agonisingly long, but it was only five minutes in reality. *What was the result? You will need to travel further. Stay with me I am counting on your support. Remember we agreed to hold hands along this journey.*

Test results were positive, the blue line remained prominent after five minutes, and I held the kit so tightly as if it were a million pounds, like gold dust that I could not allow out of my hands. I held it as if it were the very baby itself. When hubby returned home, I said, *darling, look at the results*. We are pregnant, pregnant! We laughed, we cried, and we thanked God. We stood still to savour the moment, how intimate and wonderful an experience! It was as if there was a sweet smell of roses and a bird had flown into our lives—like feathers flowing all around us, ushering in new life. At that point, our entire lives had changed, which would be challenging yet exciting. We were about to embark on the world of pregnancy/parenthood, take on the greatest responsibility—the honour to eventually become proud parents.

Grace and Guidance

We first had to overcome our own internal and external barriers, such as coming to terms with the entire pregnancy at my age. I was in my late 40s and did not actually know anyone else pregnant in this age category. This made me feel isolated and almost engendered feelings of embarrassment, particularly when attending hospital appointment, especially if hubby could not reschedule his shifts to accompany me. All the other women looked much younger.

How did I cope with this aspect of the journey? I basically accepted that God allowed us to become pregnant now. I was truly grateful and laughed in a positive sense, unlike *Sarah* in the Bible, who laughed out of disbelief. My laughter was out of joy and belief. I decided that I would enjoy this rare life-changing opportunity and think of it as an honour to serve God, to be able to bear a child in middle age. I found myself identifying with *Mary and Elizabeth* in the Bible when they became pregnant. I too sang my own song of joy, praise, and thanksgiving, to be granted this privilege that many so desperately long for.

The following challenges were not easy. I had to inform the GP, work, family, church, and close friends. We attended the GP, and they immediately assigned me a consultant. I was informed that *"you are high risk and therefore, you will need regular check-ups and stringent monitoring under the circumstances"*. I recall reminding them that *"I am not ill"*. I accept that I am older than most pregnant women, regardless. I want to be treated with the same respect and courtesy.

My employers were wonderful; they encouraged me to stop all visits to establishments that I would generally visit. In addition to providing me with a special chair, they made allowances to accommodate my fortnightly hospital appointments/check-ups. The staff ensured that I left the office on time and not late evening, as previously accustomed. My close friend and colleague were also pregnant, so we spent quality time together planning shopping trips. I recall us discussing breastfeeding and the sales at Tesco on bottles and other essential items for the baby's arrival and survival. Eleven years later, I still remember one of my colleagues' response when I told her that I was pregnant. She actually swore out of shock, but she quickly covered her mouth and apologised. She was so happy for me and actually offered me her pram, which she had stored for many years.

Friends supported me throughout the pregnancy, ensuring that I was eating well, taking exercise, resting, and reading the relevant material about babies. I recall purchasing a few baby books and a book of names, which I kept and gave to my daughter in 2019.

My family was delighted with the news. They were extremely protective, despite living outside of London. It never stopped them from holding regular check-ups via phone, visits, and conversations with each other. Mother would remind me to drink plenty of fluid and retire to bed early instead of my usual eleven o'clock.

Transformation

I initially gained weight gradually around my stomach, which was hardly noticeable for the first three months externally, but internally, everything was in motion, and I certainly felt the impact. I could not wear close-fitting clothing after two months or eat certain fruit such as bananas, which I previously loved. I could no longer bend quickly or touch my toes after four months. I could not stand strong smells such as vinegar, and even milk, which I enjoyed drinking. I did not have significant cravings for anything in particular, as some women crave unusual things such as coal or chalk. Many people recommended ginger biscuits to prevent morning sickness and nausea because of my hypersensitivity to touch, taste, smells, and hearing. I was pleased that my first three months were pain-free, with only slight discomfort to my recollection.

I found myself becoming really excited more than usual as time went by. I walked daily in the snow and did not feel tired. I recalled my younger colleague telling our manager that when she became pregnant, she should not be expected to keep up like Doreen, as her pregnancy was a miracle. I echoed that my pregnancy was miraculous, and therefore, management could not use me as a benchmark.

As time drew near, I became bigger, and walking became difficult, mainly the last two months. I wanted to stay in, relax, and eat as my heart desired. I used self-control, thinking about the impact on our baby; for example, anything questionable such as certain types of fish. Therefore, I stopped eating fresh tuna, shellfish, including prawns which I previously loved. My emotions could best be described as high as if I were floating in the air, on cloud nine for the best part of the pregnancy. It was as if God carried me, as if a chorus of angels watched over me from the inception. It was a wonderful state of tranquillity. If I accidentally offended others, I could blame it on being pregnant at my age. The downside is that one can become forgetful, brain fog, irritable, and moody. These are only a few of the symptoms I experienced, but I am sure hubby and friends could pinpoint many.

During pregnancy, one is bombarded with plenty of advice and information, all of which is intended to be supportive. To be frank, it becomes almost impossible to differentiate between fact, opinion, and fiction.

The clock is ticking; the nesting period meant that I was obsessed with cleaning items associated with the baby. I recall incessantly washing all the clothing a few weeks beforehand, cleaning the house seemingly a million times, wiping walls, doors, windows, flooring, and insisting on purchasing new things which were never used. I was prepared and ready for our little bundle of joy. My husband returned from work daily to find the hallway littered with bags of items, including bottles and a highchair, which we could not use for eight months. This was my way of preparing for all eventuality as I did not want to be taken unaware, and no one was going to stop me from enjoying the ride. Hubby took it in his stride and reminded me that we have a lifetime to purchase items for the child who will not remain a baby for long. *"The baby can only wear one suit of clothing at a time."* The baby will also receive many gifts.

Lessons Learnt from my Journey

I learnt that:

- Life is not about who you are but what and how you navigate through the course of life.
- I need others to make my world meaningful and to have a purpose.
- We are more resilient than we think we are. Once faced with challenging circumstances, we can step up to the mark with helping hands, support, and encouragement. '*We can do all things through Christ that strengths us*' (Philippians 4:13; KJV) and with positive people around us.

Practical Take-Aways

You can:

- Achieve anything you desire, and age is not a

barrier. The only barrier is usually yourself. So, pick yourself up. Use what you have!
- Encounter hurdles at any stage but leap over them with a spirit of expectancy, purpose, and awe.

Promise

...It's a girl!

A top of the morning to our bundle of joy. Welcome to the world, our world. We promise to love, cherish, and keep you safe with the support of God, family, and the community. As they say, "It takes a community to raise a child". Let's get started.

6

FROM PAIN TO PROMISE: NAVIGATING ENDOMETRIOSIS

SIMONE SCOTT-SAWYER

It was another blissfully sunny day in the motherland, perfect for a family trip to Leicester one of the rural, mountain villages in the capital. This day stands out as one of those idyllic moments frozen in time. The surroundings were lush green, providing rich playing ground for me and great habitat for animals too. The adults were indoors chattering and preparing food, but I couldn't care less because this was when time stood still. Something moved in the bushes, darting from left to right, swinging in the trees, then it descended onto the ground and shared the space which I occupied. That day I had my first encounter with a monkey and I was in love! Little old me with this creature. It took a few tentative steps towards me, seemingly curious about me, as I was about him. This started my lifelong adoration for animals, one of the many reasons why my childhood in Africa turned out to be a blessed and beautiful experience.

I first went to Freetown, Sierra Leone at the ripe old age of five and as a cheeky youngster, soon learned to survive, a bit like that monkey. When I first arrived, I was the youngest among my family members at the time and they all doted on me. I excelled at school and that kept my parents happy. Life at home was grand – my beloved grandmother of blessed memory lived with us so I had two marvellous matriarchs pouring into my life. We had home help including a driver, a maid and beloved dogs that roamed free in our compound. My mother, an educationist worked for the Institute of Education and after school I would make my way to her office. Of course I needed to get home, but playing with my pals was the more appealing prospect. Her colleagues had children my age, so after school we would all converge on the office grounds and play to our hearts' content. My father was a hotelier who managed different hotels, so at weekends my mother and I would often take a drive and join him for lunch or dinner. My favourite spot was when he worked for a popular hotel resort called Lagoonda as it overlooked a lagoon. It comprised three restaurants, a cinema and a casino. I was fortunate being exposed to that lifestyle at such a young age.

The Joys of Womanhood?

The only blot on this beautiful picture I have painted, was an insatiable need to grow up, because although my childhood was sweet, I longed to become an adult. Typical right! My parents were super strict so I figured that once I was a grown woman, things would be different. It didn't really change things but that was beside the point. All my girlfriends seemed to be 'filling out' and this seemed to magically happen around puberty. I had a strong desire to graduate from girlhood to womanhood. I was always a skinny little mini growing up and had observed many of my friends blossom into attractive, voluptuous women. In my mind, a *woman,* meant being curvy and sassy and this made her sexy and appealing and it seemed that puberty was the gateway to womanhood. I was overjoyed to be escorting my mother to the chemist to purchase sanitary products and would roll my eyes back and pretend to bemoan the fact that periods always arrived at the most inopportune time like sports days at school. So, when I started experiencing monthly, excruciating and nauseating pain with my periods, you can imagine the horror I felt, wondering why me? I pondered: was this the price of womanhood? Finding out from some of my friends that menstruation was the most unremarkable thing happening to them left me perplexed. Why all the drama with me? Feeling like a freak, every time my period started, my life stopped, literally. I missed school, my mother would mop my fevered brow and nurse me back to health, comforting me by telling me it would get better. Only it would not. If anything, things got progressively worse.

Living with Pain

Many years later, back in the UK, I would come to describe my condition as: at best, each month, the pain was so debilitating that I would virtually pass out, and at worst, I ended up in pain every single day, culminating in me being rushed to my local Accident and Emergency department by ambulance to be put on morphine. Imagine that! All because I was on my period.

It just so happened that this horror began to unfold around a time in my life supposed to be my happiest. The man I was madly in love with at the time, had whisked me off to a beautiful restaurant in London's West End on my birthday. He decided to propose to me, in the middle of the restaurant catching me completely off guard. I remember a total sense of oneness I felt that day - I am big on birthdays and the day was perfectly planned. I had taken the day off work, pampered myself all day and had the rest of the night to take the birthday celebrations to a different level. However, I was also on my period on that day. To tell the truth, most of the pampering was devoted to pain management as was the norm whenever my unwelcome monthly visitor appeared. This was standard practice when I had diary events which coincided with my period as I would need to plan around the events. So, if I was being whisked away somewhere fancy that evening, I needed time to sort myself out. I needed to relax mentally and physically and put myself in a zone where I was as close to pain-free as possible. This typically meant a super-hot shower, plenty of hot drinks throughout the day, relaxing music and most important of all, lots of strong painkillers. These included Co-codamol, Tramadol and Diclofenac. I also used Temgesic a super-strong, sublingual analgesic, which administered a slow release of synthetic morphine under my tongue, usually leaving me zonked for significant periods. Ordinarily this kept me sedated, but this was no ordinary day.

There were seven courses and I remember somewhere around course three, my then partner coming around the table to my side and all of a sudden, he dropped to one knee and popped the question! I went into slow motion mode where my brain needed to catch up with what had just happened. It seemed however the rest of the diners had figured this out before me and started to murmur and cheer. I noticed the heads turning, the smiles and then realised what was occurring and was over the moon. Almost immediately after that glorious moment, things took a drastically, different turn. My stomach suddenly went into overdrive and what started as light cramps intensified and I felt like I was about to pass out. Due to the intensity of the pain, I always prayed such episodes happened at home, so I could take measures to alleviate the pain. This included taking inertia inducing analgesics and willing myself to sleep so I felt no pain. Having an attack whilst out in public, complicated things as I was always mindful I needed to conduct myself accordingly, when all I wanted to do was curl up in a ball and scream. So on this occasion I headed to the bathroom, it was a drill I was familiar with. The pain was so debilitating, that I virtually lost the ability to stand up. This was nothing new, but sadly I was in a public space and had just gotten engaged. I was or at least should have been on cloud nine, but I wasn't. Once I used the bathroom, I could envisage the usual pain-train hurtling towards me once again, about to mow me down in its track. I ended up collapsing into a heap on the floor, that familiar pain gripped my entire body with such overwhelming, convulsing intensity, I dare not move. Incapacitated by the pain, I was curled up in a ball in a public loo, now what? I had to call for assistance from one of the staff members, who kindly escorted me back to my table. I remember the confused looks all around as we made a hasty retreat and hopped into a black cab, abruptly cutting short the night. I never thought it was possible to feel deflated and inflated all at once.

What I had not realised at the time, was although I had learnt to hobble along with the crippling, monthly pain for years, this latest episode was more indicative of a deeper malaise worsening inside my body. Unbeknown to me, what had been dismissed for years as just 'painful periods' was because of a medically recognised condition. For decades I was left feeling like a hypochondriac after different doctors said it was normal to have period pains and I simply had to bear it. That is until the day I was rushed to the A & E department after collapsing in pain. The pain was so severe that I was immediately given morphine on admission. Several A & E trips later, the baffled consultants finally decided it was time to go in. Surgery was recommended and a laparoscopy performed. Finally, I had a diagnosis, Endometriosis, some 16 years later! It actually came as a relief.

For some unknown reason the condition causes cells and tissues found in the endometrium to migrate and attach themselves to other vital organs in the woman's body, including the bowels, ovaries and even the lungs. Each month when menstruation occurs, as they have no point of escape, they harden and form tumours and cysts and cause untold pain. Hence my worst nightmare culminating and coinciding with one of the best points in my life. Being a degenerative condition meant the misdiagnoses allowed it to worsen. The Endometriosis simply overtook my body like a juggernaut from hell. I succumbed and ended up at the mercy of my medical team who desperately sought a solution. They had hoped that during the laparoscopy they'd be able to excise the endometrial tissues, but unfortunately like tumours, the growths had invaded large sections of my body including my bowels. This necessitated major surgery and although I was petrified, as the pain was all-pervasive, I had no choice. My life rapidly evolved into a revolving door of endless hospital appointments for tests, pre-surgery checks and procedures. My gynaecologist collaborated with a bowel surgeon and both would perform the operation. A major resection of my bowels through a laparotomy was required and I was advised that should things go wrong I could end up with an ileostomy bag, for life! I remember feeling like I was outside my body receiving this news and immediately rejecting the possibility. Though petrified, I willed myself through the process and like a lamb to the slaughterhouse agreed to the surgery. The morning of the operation felt surreal. My parents ever present, were worried sick. The sheer scale of the surgery, whether it would succeed or not and going under general anaesthetic troubled us all. I remember the best part of that day was being given anaesthetic and being asked to count down from 10 down to 1 as it was being administered. I got as far as seven and I was out. The next thing I remember was hearing my name being called out, being asked to wake up in a very cold room and feeling very irritated. Little did I know that this would be the least of my troubles.

Once I came to, the first thing I did was check to ensure there was no bag. I placed my hand on my tummy, no bag. Thank God! I drifted in and out of deep sleep that day but ended up very poorly. I was connected to myriad of tubes, my blood pressure kept dropping and unknown to me at the time, certain parts of my body had stopped working. Over the ensuing days things needed to 'settle down' and 24 hour bed rest was advised. Post-surgery pain is on another level, so I was permanently attached to a morphine pump. My medical team would do morning rounds, updating me on progress and why I needed to remain bed bound. After a week a physiotherapist was recommended to help with my mobility. My mobility? What on earth for? As I had been confined to my bed for some time, I was told I would need some assistance getting out and walking. It made no sense to me, that is until the day when I attempted to get out of bed and walk and nearly collapsed in the process. That was when I realised what a complex machinery the human body is. Being in one position for so long after my insides had been tinkered with, mixed with a combination of powerful analgesics, meant I had to learn to walk again. There was worse to come. As the tubes were systematically disconnected, it transpired that my bladder had ceased working. The consultants couldn't fathom what went wrong. I was fitted with an in-dwelling catheter just prior to my discharge and warned it may become a permanent fixture.

It was bewildering having urine retention and using a catheter, but I was relieved to be back at my parents convalescing in the privacy of my home. My appetite slowly returned as I delighted in my mother's home cooked food once again, no more hospital food. Then just as I was adjusting to my new reality of self-catheterising whilst convalescing, praying that my bladder would start to function again, bang! Things took a very sinister turn. I woke up one morning and just did not feel right. Something had gone wrong with my organs. The point where my bowels had been re-sectioned, ruptured and I got very sick. I was rushed back into hospital and my worst fears materialised. The bowels sutures broke and yes, in order to allow that area to be repaired and heal, I needed a bag. Although the consultant was hopeful it would be a temporary thing, they warned that if the surgery was unsuccessful, it could become permanent. Again, I remember immediately rejecting that possibility. However, this was not easy news to digest. Yet more surgery and an ileostomy was performed to attach a bag to my small bowel called the ileum. This is called a stoma. I was taught how to care for the stoma every day and was regularly in and out of hospital for consultations.

There were lots of bad days following the creation of my stoma. Though I embraced my stoma care routine, I struggled mentally and psychologically. My altered body image left me angry and frustrated, but above all scared about how my future might look. My body was barely functioning as a human, much less a woman. I needed bags to assist with basic bodily functions and in my dark moments, wondered when life would be good again. I went off my food, my weight plummeted and at one point was advised by my medical team that if I didn't start eating properly I would be admitted to hospital again and force fed! Well, that was the wakeup call I needed. Suddenly I woke up one day in tears and remembered who Simone was and realised that Simone the patient was not me. The thought of going back inside was abhorrent to me and the catalyst which switched my mind from 'woe is me' to 'what a wonder the human body is'. I became curious and started to marvel at how my body was functioning despite its temporary limitations. Once I began to feel gratitude, my attitude changed and my healing began. With my mindset in the right place, focusing on what I needed to get myself back on track, slowly but surely, I was able to reverse my situation.

Purpose from Pain

A year later, following the extensive surgery and complications the pain returned as the condition has no cure. I was told my best option was monthly pain management, which meant reliance on strong painkillers. Once again, I rejected that notion and embarked on another journey to find a solution. There was a time when it felt like the condition defined my world and I needed to regain control.

What a beautiful day that was, when purely through serendipity, I was introduced to a Flower Essence specialist who effectively helped me reverse the horrendous symptoms and gave me back my quality of life. Furthermore, following a spell of self-discovery through personal and professional development, I learnt to break through some self-imposed barriers and started vlogging about my Endometriosis battle on my YouTube channel. Supporting other sufferers on their lonesome journey is incredibly gratifying.

That inner fortitude and faith I discovered also emboldened me to make further changes in my professional life. Turning my pain into my passion by sharing my health woes with the world allowed me to press further into those latent gifts and talents I have. Today I use my legal skills and training coupled with my creative aptitude to write, use my voice and present content in various media among others. Poor health can be such an impediment to pursuing ones goals, and being released from those shackles is the greatest blessing.

7

THE PAIN OF SUSPENDING GRIEF: NAVIGATING GRIEF

PAULINE MCFARLANE

Lying in my bed on a cold November morning, a glimmer of the uninviting grey clouds peered through the small gap where the curtains meet. I was crippled with pain in every fibre of my being, with stiff joints that would take a miracle to unlock. Crying out in excruciating, maddening, unimaginable pain, I couldn't help but ask how I ended up like this. I'm not a bad person; I haven't caused any harm to others. I haven't ignored the cries, pleas, and distress of others. I haven't abandoned those who so needed and relied upon me any time or day. No, I haven't!

On the contrary, I have given selflessly of my time and energy to the point of suspending my own emotional distress for a long, and I mean, a very long time. I did this to support and show the love and care that has been asked, no not asked, demanded of me. I have jumped to answer others' needs, regardless of what my own physical, spiritual, and emotional needs required. I had a total neglect of self, yet I thought that I was doing the right thing—the honourable thing, the loving, dutiful thing by giving myself to others. Others, who I now know, as I lay here lonely, afraid, despondent, distressed, disappointed, and in so much pain, did not care for me in the slightest. What a heartbreaking realisation that is rocking me to the core of my very being! I do not think I could hurt or feel any more pain. I am numb.

What has brought me to this place, you ask? Well, I found myself amid a protracted acrimonious divorce, which should have been over way long ago, from my decision to divorce. I struggled to absorb this daily trauma, humiliation, and sheer distress whilst trying to keep on top of my highly stressful job and raising my family. Amid this, I watched helplessly as my aged parents' infirmities ate away at their being until they eventually faded away and drew their last breath. Every fibre of my being silently screamed out. My mother has died, same with my father, and my siblings are now scattered—no glue to hold us together anymore. Yet, to those around me, it is as if I remained untouched. *"No care required there"*, I imagine their thoughts.

My attempts to seek support by subtly indicating that I was not okay fell on deaf ears. I could hear the cold silence and disinterest through the phone. No feedback; no confirmation that my feelings were real. No concern, no support, not even a celebratory acknowledgement of my successes in the face of adversities. Just silence. I realised that they were unable, incapable, or unwilling to give of themselves, to reciprocate.

The luxury of a space to speak and be heard was not to be for me. At times, I wanted to scream, *"What about me!? I need help; can't you see that?"* This would swiftly be followed by me swallowing my internal exclamations with a drink of guilt and shame for thinking such selfish thoughts. Could I not see that other people were in distress and crying out for my undivided attention? *"My problems and concerns were not that important; I can cope"*, I would admonish myself. I was overly attuned to the needs of the people around me, who demanded their right to comfort, encouragement, and attention.

I have to let you know that this illness did not come overnight. My body, the precious and caring being that it is, had spent the previous few years sending signs and signals that something was not right. The subtle suggestions started with my digestive system holding on to consumed food, refusing to let it pass through my system, refusing to let it go. This was followed by the unexplained pains in my lower back, neck, and soles of my feet. I felt as though I was falling apart, but I kept it moving. The determined soul that I was found a way around this continuing on my merry way.

I realise now that this was all a defence mechanism. By being so invested in supporting others, I was delaying and suspending the inevitable pain of grief. I had shown up consistently, never missing or dropping a call, not even when I was crying inside. My only outlet was finding a safe and quiet space when the enormity of grief that I could no longer contain flooded my soul. I would break down and cry. The delaying of grief had brought me to my knees. No, in fact, it literally knocked me off my feet. I no longer had a choice but to be still.

"You have a condition called Polymyalgia Rheumatica—PMR", the kind-looking Rheumatologist advised me as I sat quietly expectantly in his bright but sterile office on a chilly January morning. *"It's an autoimmune disease, and we don't know what causes this, but we do know that more women than men are diagnosed with this". Oh my God, what is that? Am I going to die? Is there a cure?* My mind raced with a multitude of questions. As I scanned my mind, visualising several scenarios, none of them ending well for me. *What's going to happen to my children? Will I live long enough to be able to enjoy my grandchild, to watch him grow?* At that moment, I knew…I came to the stark realisation that I was never in control. I was never in control of my emotional distress, rationalising to myself that I was in control of all the grief which had piled up one on top of the other over the years.

I instinctively knew that my unresolved grief and lack of connection with this natural emotion was a contributory factor to the grief showing up in my body as PMR—the cause of this unbearable pain throughout my muscles, stiffness in my joints, chronic fatigue, and a whole host of emotional symptoms all contriving to bring me down. My body and mind had had enough and shut down. I needed to grieve and heal.

I could barely hear the Consultant's words as he attempted to explain, *"We can treat the symptoms, it will take a couple of years to get under control, but the prognosis is good"*. I realised at that moment that I was holding my breath and so let out a gasp of relief as my thoughts of doom slowly ebbed away.

So, here I find myself a month later, wrapped in a towel sitting in the steam room of this luxurious spa hotel, feeling defeated, uncomfortable, and in pain. I tried to figure out how I can nourish my body to hurry the healing process, as I did not believe that medication alone was the way to go. Having tried a range of vitamins and minerals bought after my extensive internet search, I really am uncertain of what I was doing. I'm not a nutritionist, so was I causing more harm to my body? I felt confused and despondent. *"God, help me. I don't know what to do; I need help"*, I cried softly to myself, as the hot drips of water landed on my shoulder, bringing me back to reality. Feeling drained and forlorn, I made my way back to the reception area to return my towel. *"So, what brings you here?"* said the bright-eyed young receptionist in that annoying, upbeat. I'm so fit and happy I could burst voice. I am instantly annoyed. *"Well, my daughter has invited me to come and spend some time with her here in the hotel"*. *"Oh?"* she inquired, wanting me to elaborate. I silently rolled my eyes and reluctantly added, *"I've been unwell for a while now, and she thought that a change of scenery and some pampering would cheer me up"*, I reluctantly added, not really wanting to engage in any superficial chit chat. *"Oh, so what's the matter?"* she persisted, with a look of genuine concern in her eyes. I braced myself for the monologue I had become used to and launched into relaying my ill-health journey leading to my diagnosis. Whilst doing so, I noticed a young man sitting in a room behind the young lady. I could see he was positioning himself listening in on our conversation. He slowly spun his chair around to face me, rose, and came to the reception desk. *"Oh boy, here we go, another fit and healthy soul coming over to chat"*, I thought, by this time wanting to beat a hasty retreat. He introduced himself, and we started to talk about my diagnosis. As a fitness and health specialist, he was keen to hear more about my journey and what I was doing to aid my recovery. We talked and laughed, and then he told me about a friend who had an autoimmune condition who had seen a well-respected nutritionist in Harley Street. I heard the words Harley Street and shut down momentarily. *"Please, who's got money to spend in Harley Street?"* And before I could finish my musings, he had opened his laptop and navigated to the nutritionist's website. Together, we scanned through the information, where I read about the types of patients treated and some insightful testimonials. By this point, I wasn't even concerned about the cost. Just knowing that someone was out there who understood and could treat my condition was priceless to me. The young man wrote it down and handed me the contact details on a piece of paper, which I took and eagerly tucked away in the pocket of my oversized white soft robe. I felt that I had skipped back to my room, excited and with renewed hope.

So, what did I learn from this experience? One of the lessons I have learnt is that God answered my prayers in the most unexpected way. I learnt that God had never taken His gaze off me and that He only required that I ask for help and have faith that it will be done. I realised that God would take care of me if I allowed Him to. I do not have to do it all on my own. I see how much easier it is to trust that our Creator loves us unconditionally and at all times, despite the twists and turns we take in life. God has the power to make our crooked path straight. I have been fighting against God, using whatever means to defend against the all-consuming pain of grief and refusing to allow myself to be vulnerable.

I have learnt that we are all here to serve. Angels, who are our Divine Helpers, are everywhere and will appear when you need them to help you along your journey. You just have to ask and believe. I met so many Angels along my road to recovery who came to my aid, not requiring much from me but delighted in any help and support they could give to bring a smile back to my face. I learnt that Angels appear for a designated purpose—showing up for a season or a reason. It is important to recognise that they will naturally fade away from your life when they have fulfilled their purpose. The mistake is that we can sometimes try to hold on to these Angels because we want them to stay in our lives, to be a helper, friend, ally, partner, or even as a substitute parent. This is not their purpose. These Angels may not even be aware of why they have been drawn to you, but they have followed their spirit—the word of God without question, in order to do His will, serve, help, and heal. So, bless them and let them go; grieve the loss and move on.

I have learnt that letting go allows others to stand on their own two feet. It allows them to discover their own hidden talents, resilience, interests, and strengths that will serve them more than my personal sacrifice could have ever hoped to achieve. It opens them up to experiences and opportunities to achieve their goals and potential. It may also give them the space to consider their own self-limiting beliefs, to hear their own negative chatter and a chance to correct this if they choose. Looking at it this way, you will then question who am I to stand in the way of God's purpose for their lives? I really don't want to be trying to block God's work!

Letting go means the energy and focus can now return to you. You are free and able to open up a spiritual space to let God enter your life, work His miracles, free up space for you to dream without boundaries or limitations, and dream beyond your wildest imagination. Letting go will also enable you to soar high up amongst the clouds in the skies, dream of infinite possibilities for your life and about your future, causing you to be free from the shackles of guilt and shame that has held you back. Letting go trains you to be still, know, listen, and hear the quiet gentle voice from within, which has so often either gone unheard or challenged. That voice which says, *"I matter"*.

Letting go allows the space for new beginnings and new people to come into your life. It allows you to live on purpose, to set your intentions and revel in the happiness that is peace. I have learnt that peace repairs all the shattered pieces. It is the peace in Christ that has restored my health. It was from this space where I was able to birth my Company, McFarlane & Associates Ltd - *Transformation Through Conversation,* a Personal and Professional consultancy business, where I am privileged to support clients through Coaching and Mentoring sessions to identify, achieve their goals, and aspirations. It is here where I really come alive. The immense satisfaction I receive from playing a part in transforming lives is immeasurable.

I also learnt the importance of knowing that you are precious, that you matter, and your needs matter. Know that you are perfectly and wonderfully made. God designs you with gifts to realise His purpose. You have work to do, and so a focus on your health and wellbeing is non-negotiable. This means creating and communicating your boundaries—no more people-pleasing; no more playing small to make others feel tall.

It is super important to surround yourself with people who care, love, and support you. Find people you can trust—a confidante, that go-to sister who you know talks a lot of sense which comes from wisdom and isn't afraid to check you when you are spiralling out of control. Nurture these relationships; they need to be nourished and refreshed and you also need to give of yourself. Do what you can to reciprocate. Sometimes as a Giver, it can feel quite uncomfortable to take from others, but know that your emotional tank or bucket needs to be filled with fresh energy. It is crucial to understand the needs of your mind, body, and spirit. Notice when there is a dip in energy. Notice when you need quiet time and space to recharge, or indeed when you need to be out and about socialising or having a good time. It is okay to have self-love; scrap that; it is essential. Self-love is not selfishness. It is putting the world on notice that you value yourself, which means taking care of yourself.

Taking time out gives you the space to figure out in your own time who you truly are and what your divine purpose is. You are more able to align with your purpose and have conviction in your gifts. You can envisage how you are going to share, teach, and serve through your gifts. How amazing is that! What a liberation, what a revelation when you know that you have a divine assignment! You realise that your life does have meaning and purpose. You acknowledge that the uncertainties, anxieties, and those nagging negative thoughts are just an illusion.

Today, my health is much improved. I no longer rely on the medication nor on the numerous nutritional supplements that have helped restore me to good health. The physical and emotional manifestations of this debilitating disease are now gone. I have never felt healthier and more alive. I have learnt that loss and grief are necessary in life because as the seasons change, we too, as humans, will change.

I give thanks for all the lessons I have learned through this challenging time in my life. I give thanks for all the opportunities to create, open my heart, see, and let in those who genuinely care for me. I give thanks for this valuable and life-transforming lesson about the pain of suspended grief. I hope you will gain something from my life lessons that will support you along your journey.

8

FINDING NEW LIFE AFTER LEUKEMIA: NAVIGATING MY DIAGNOSIS

PRECIOUS JASON

My dear friend,

On the 2nd June 2012, at about 7 p.m. British time, I had the good fortune of hearing five words no one should have to hear.

"Meez Jah son, you have cancer".

Fortune you say? Bear with me.

On that day, I felt anything but fortunate. In fact, when the bearer of the news delivered those five, little punch-packed words in a strong and cute Bengali accent, my entire world collapsed.

I was torn between wailing and laughing hysterically. I choose the latter because it all sounded ridiculous and stupid.

A few hours earlier, I had been on my way to teach a business student preparing for her A levels, and all I could think about on the tube journey was how to deliver my lesson and have the rest of the Saturday off.

"Cancer? As in ***the*** *cancer?"* I gasped.

Cancer happened to other people. I didn't know anyone directly who had such a thing. I mean I had heard of people who had been diagnosed, and I had put them on my prayer lists and left it at that. I was one of those people. I knew sod all.

I remember one time I did a race for life event in Hyde park with my girlfriend, Bunmi. We were given name tags and asked to write down who we were running for. I suppose it was to make the race more meaningful. I watched on as people noted their mums, sisters, and girlfriends and realised I didn't have any names to hand, so I quickly scribbled *"for everyone affected by cancer"* and joined the race.

"Mrs Jah son. Can you hear me?"

Nod.

"We have had your blood test back. Your symptoms indicate you have Leukaemia—a blood cancer. The good news is of all the cancers you can possibly have, this one is the best. You only have to take medication. You are truly fortunate," he beamed.

You know those movies where a person dies and steps out of their body and looks in shock? That was me. I mean, jokes aside, how the heck does blood have cancer? What would they be cutting off exactly?

The interesting thing was I had heard about my diagnosis an hour before the hospital doctor broke the news, but for some reason, getting it from an official source made it real. Ridiculous, yes. Real, yes too.

En route to my job that morning, I alighted at Hampstead tube station in London and had managed to faint near the ticket gates which set off the chain of events. I love a bit of drama in real life, so I am not surprised that the drama found me on this auspicious occasion.

A lovely Nigerian man who worked in the station called an ambulance, and I grudgingly got in, clueless about what lay ahead. I was in a lot of pain that day and the train journey had been an uncomfortable one, but the last place I wanted to be on a Saturday was a hospital. However, passing out so dramatically shook me a bit and I decided it was best to get help.

I called my brother Andy when I got to A&E to let him know where I was. He arrived with his wife a few hours later to my relief. My sister-in-law, Kemi, is a medical doctor, so I was grateful to have her while we prayed and nervously waited in our semiprivate cubicle. I was a bit upset at having to spend the day in hospital but secretly grateful I was getting much-needed care. I would be able to get to the root of the problem here.

We were unprepared when Kemi came into the cubicle a few hours later, ashen-faced. I watched as she whispered to Andrew and his face crumpled. They both sat on my bed and held my hands.

"How are you feeling, Pre?"

"A bit better", I mumbled.

"Pre, we know what is wrong. I overheard the doctors at the station. Would you like me to tell you, or would you like them to tell you?" Her eyes were lowered.

I nodded. It would be better coming from them.

"They think you have cancer".

Mmm...okay. That can't be. In Christianese, it was not my portion. We prayed anyway, and I boldly declared that I would come out of "whatever-this-was-in-the-name-of-Jesus-amen" unscathed.

Nah man, Kemi must have heard wrong. As much as I loved her, I secretly hoped she had misheard. I mean, I probably had a kidney infection as my kidney (on the lower left side of my abdomen) was swollen and sore. I failed biology first time, bear with me.

I had been unwell for some months. I was constantly fighting one infection or the other. I had bruises all over my body, massive lumps under my armpit and neck, and I was constantly tired. All the classic signs were there but sadly, they were not picked up.

I had done all the right things. I had been to see my GP several times and each time, he would put me on a course of antibiotics, each one stronger than the last and tell me to stop working so hard. There was a day I stood in the reception, prescription in hand and I wailed. I knew instinctively something was wrong but felt unable to question Dr Makanji's diagnosis. He robustly assured me that I was dealing with stress and I went home and rested as instructed. He was the doctor, and I the patient. So, I had no choice but to believe him even though my mind knew I was not okay.

And yet, here I was in A&E, a few months down the line, staring at a man with a funny accent, telling me I had cancer. If he called me Mrs Jah-son one more time, I would punch him in the face.

Dr B or Shiv as he liked to be called, had lied to me.

I was in the Royal Free Hospital for months. Once they had found me a bed that night, I commenced treatment and eventually found out I had chronic myeloid leukaemia, an unusual cancer of the white blood cells (who knew). My white blood cells were ridiculously high, and it turned out the swollen bit on the bottom left side of my abdomen was my spleen.

I started on medication as Shiv had said, then onto chemotherapy, total body radiation and finally a stem cell transplant as the disease morphed between phases. In that time, Shiv discovered my real name was Precious, and we became good friends.

The treatment was gruelling, and it took its toll on my body, mind, and spirit and although I tried to keep a brave face, I was struggling on every side. At the start of the process, I was a healthy size 14, with a full head of hair, energy, and dream. Heck, I even had long-term plans. By the end of a whole year of active treatment, I was charred, bald, a size 8, broken, and deflated. Now, my longest life plan was making it through the hour.

I remember being discharged after the transplant with three bags of medication, manuals, and a list of numbers to call in case something went wrong and wondering what to do with the rest of my life.

I was scared mad. Mad at God and madder at life. I didn't want to live, which was ironic considering I had put myself through all that treatment in order to live.

What kind of God would allow His child to go through such a terrible time? Where was the love in that? Where was the goodness everyone banged on about? I was a bundle of anger and frustration. I used to go for walks at 2 a.m. to yell and scream at my misfortune, expressing my anger without caring for my safety.

"What would become of me?"

"Where do I begin?"

"What was all that about? I am done with this Christianity thing. It is useless".

With tears streaming down my face, I would wearily trudge home by dawn and collapse into bed to grab sleep and repeat the cycle. I don't know why that was a thing then, but I think it did me good to vent even though it was a silly thing to walk alone in the dead of the night. Looking back, I am thankful for protection in that period.

A New Perspective

Over time, I healed. One thing I had going for me was the love of an amazing family and friends, and they loved hard. They did not always have answers, but I know they were praying for me while I did my best to navigate life from the ashes. I also had an excellent team of professionals and therapists who encouraged me to try little things to get going.

"Find a charity; they always need people. Date. Travel. Learn a new language. Write".

I went one extra. I went on dates, travelled with total strangers to unusual places, joined a choir, did a skydive, took a French class, got a puppy, volunteered, and started a business.

I don't remember how I discovered a foodbank near my flat, but I was thrilled to have something meaningful to do, and I loved talking to the clients and working with Pat, Christina, and Lisa—the wonderful women who ran the foodbank.

One day, conversation turned to church and someone asked if I would like to attend (the church ran the foodbank, and the building was used for services during the week). I had no intention of returning to God. Our contract had long expired.

I am grateful for the wonderful people who never pushed but shared their struggles with me and how their faith guided them. There were everyday people who just loved, who cared about making things right. No fireworks, just everyday living. Extraordinary acts done in the gentlest of ways.

With time, I began to pray again and relearn a few things about life, love, and faith. It has been several years since I first walked into the foodbank and my life has not been the same. I continue to be inspired by their service and commitment to making people's lives better.

One of the side effects of the treatment was dry, damaged skin and severe hair loss. I once attended a charity beauty event for women dealing with cancer treatment and we were given makeup bags with a lot of beauty products and taught how to wear makeup. Although I was extremely grateful for the goody bag and that people were thinking of cancer patients who often felt forgotten, the expensive products irritated my already sensitive skin. I had issues finding natural products that would soothe my skin without causing more problems.

A New Season

Noticing a gap in the market and having time on my hands, I created a natural skincare brand for post-cancer treatment damaged skin and hair. I wanted to change the narrative and was extremely grateful to have won multiple awards, get featured in the press (the serious ones), invited to No.10 Downing Street, and asked to speak at the legit business events, sometimes in front of people who knew what they were doing. I was always amused when people queued up after my talks to speak with me and ask questions. I was still trying to figure out myself behind the scenes.

On the outside, I was thriving or as I like to call it, a **survivor thriver.** On the inside, I was not doing so well. I was dealing with my health challenges behind the scenes. Sometimes, rolling from receiving an award or a standing ovation on stage to a consulting room without the different audiences knowing where I had just been. One time, I managed to get diagnosed with chronic fatigue syndrome and rolled into a new full-time job the next morning without acknowledging the news to myself or anyone else, all because I wanted to be a super strong woman bouncing back from adversity and slaying it. It didn't end well.

One day, my survivor thriver life came tumbling down and showed up in warning signs that made me take a step back and reassess my priorities just in time for the pandemic that shook us all up.

I was initially very anxious. We all were. I have had to shield for the best part of the year because of my health. I saw the forced stop of the pandemic as an opportunity to slow down and reboot. I have made some major changes in the last year. I closed the business down, resigned from a job I was unhappy in, got a job in the third sector, surrounded myself with amazing women, took a theology class, became an ambassador for a national charity (where I talk about my experience and how to improve engagement for cancer patients in the BAME community), invested in therapy for my mental health, grew my own food, and I am currently writing my memoirs (hoping to publish by the end of the year). I am also learning to breathe too in case you were wondering.

Looking back over the years, I genuinely don't have answers about the whys and the hows. The disease itself is not the good fortune leukaemia tends to be marketed as, but I would like to think that I am a better person because of my experience. The experience has made me focus on joy in the littlest things from listening to birdsong at dawn to discovering different varieties of a rose. I appreciate life more and care about making a difference to others.

Had I not been through the experience, I don't think I would have known that the chances of getting a stem cell donor match as a BAME person is very low. A few years ago, I was on the stem cell register, desperately waiting for a match only to learn about the odds stacked against our community. **We** make up just 15% of the **bone marrow** donor **register.** This means that **we** have only a 20.5% chance of finding the best possible donor match compared to 69% of our Northern European counterparts (*Figures from Anthony Nolan*). It is a sobering thought.

I eventually went on to join a clinical trial where I underwent a haploid identical stem cell transplant with stem cells from my brother, which literally saved my life. Not everyone is as lucky. What I learned in my dark times has shaped the way I live and work. I have discovered that I am resilient, courageous, and stronger than I give myself credit for, and I am extremely passionate about educating people and changing the narrative so that the people after me can get better support.

I know now that God never said it would be easy. The Bible says in **Matthew chapter 5 v 45 (NIV)**:

"He causes his sun to rise on the evil and the good and sends rain on the righteous and the unrighteous."

As a Christian, I am not immune from the challenges of life. What matters is that I know God will walk every step with me. Looking back, I can see that He was there every single minute—the minutes I acknowledged Him and those I did not. I like to think I slept in the arms of a loving father every night. Like the song that says, *"Even when I don't see it, He is working"*. I believe He has always been at work and nothing I went through will go to waste. My hope is that someone will read my story and gain strength to keep going. That will count for something; for me, that will be a life well lived.

Cancer is not something I would wish on anyone. It is not an easy journey. I continue to pray for a breakthrough in science and a cure not just for cancer but for any disease, physical or mental. I pray that anyone going through a tough season will know they are not alone and most importantly that they are loved beyond measure. Any trials that come your way will pass. I call my trials the lemon seeds of life as they have potential to birth a new tree which is a new chapter or a rebirth and as uncomfortable and painful as the process has been, I do a little growing every time.

My prayer for you, my dear friend, is no matter what you must face in this life, that you have the strength, grace, and courage to go through it with faith, hope, love, and laughter.

Love,

P x

9

REFRAMING LOSS: NAVIGATING LOSS AND ACCEPTANCE

GLYNIS BREWSTER

The aim of this story is to share a journey of pain that was initiated by the loss of a precious soul that blossoms into an amazing experience. This story demonstrates how our Heavenly Father does amazing work even through our darkest times.

In the midst of a global pandemic, I wake one morning to a loud thought: "*This book is not for me. With so many people hurting at this time due to loss, it is not okay to withhold anything that may be useful to help others navigate their own journey of despair or loss*".

God's grace has given me a gift of empathy around loss that I feel called to share. Allow me to ask you this question. Can we always reframe our losses?

1999: Drowning In Pain

My journey began in February 1999 when I was suddenly thrown into an abyss of pain and disorientation. I was informed that my only son, Sheldon, who I had spoken to less than 24 hours prior, had been taken to the hospital, where he died. I screamed and started to stammer; my brain scrambled, and my hormonal system took a hit—hello menopause!

For over two years, his death was investigated as a murder. The process was arduous; the outcome left me in limbo. Not knowing how he passed away left me with relentless questions. How and why has this happened? Was he kidnapped because he knew something? Is this another hate crime like Stephen Lawrence? Sheldon wanted to get engaged to his girlfriend, Corin, but did he feel so disappointed with life at that time that he decided to take his own life? Did his friends set him up? How could it be that nobody knew anything that would lead to how or why he died? Which of the three coroner reports were correct? Why did God let this happen? Is this some kind of test or punishment for me? Did God even care?

These questions lived with me on loudspeaker for the next 15 years.

In addition to the daily haunt of despair about his passing, every January also brought the dread of counting another year in the prison of not knowing what happened and guilt about not being present when he died.

People often asked how I was coping. *"I'm getting by"*, I'd politely respond to conceal the cesspit of pain that I was quietly drowning in. "*God knows best. God is in control; accept my condolences*" were the kind of platitudes some offered in an attempt to be respectful or comforting. They didn't know that I wished they would choke on those words as I certainly didn't want to hear them.

2003

New life arrives in our family via a boy-girl twin. My dear supportive daughter needs me. Has Sheldon come back to us via his nephew? No! I scolded myself. This is my second grandson. More questions about possible life after death arose from time to time, but I managed to get stuck into the joy of supporting new life. '*Am I worthy or qualified to do this having lost my son? How could I positively contribute after not being able to prevent such a disaster? How did I help my son during his 21 years? What evidence do I have that I mothered him well?*'

2005

The unresolved nature around this loss produces the feeling that I am being persecuted by my own mind; getting this to stop feels impossible. I'm now faced with twin toddlers to help care for at home, a daughter that needs my support, a man who would like to marry me while also having the opportunity to work with an audience of hundreds of youths weekly. Do people really not see what a big failure I have been? Is pity so blinding? It seems our resilience in handling challenges depends on our emotional tools. I found myself in a quandary with my emotional tools, most of which were influenced by my religious beliefs. Were these the correct tools, and would they work in this situation? More questions! NO MORE QUESTIONS!!

"That's it!" I decided one day. I'm not dealing with any more questions connected or associated in any way with Sheldon's passing! I was disappointed that I had not received any positive spiritual results that I could recognise so far.

But, at this moment, I realised that if I was still so angry with God, I must believe that He still existed.

So, with that, I decided to talk to Him directly and honestly:

"Father, I am broken, disappointed, and very angry with myself for not being able to protect my son, and I'm also angry with you for allowing this to happen to him. I don't know what to think anymore, and I'm tired of man's interpretations of your way and what you want of us. I AM DONE! NO MORE! I will not allow anyone else to tell me about you and your ways, so don't send them. You know me better than anyone else, and the fact that I feel this way about you means I still believe that you exist, so I am putting this disastrous experience in your hands. Whether I live or die is all with you. Whether I find out what happened to my son or not is also all with you. I'm done! If you really have a purpose for me, then show me very clearly but do it yourself. Send nobody—I will not listen to them."

This is the first decision that I made.

Since then, I was left with my memories of Sheldon and the comfort I got in revisiting those memories.

Sheldon had left three children. What would he have wanted or expected that I do with them? That was going to be a battle, as I also wondered if any of their mothers had a direct or indirect connection to his passing. I decided I would love them without being interrupted by doubt. This would prove a bit more difficult with one of the two little girls. I'd only seen her twice and had no idea where she was. Her name is Candace.

I had been praying for her safety and to find her, but as the years went by, it felt increasingly unlikely. I wondered if she was living in the north of England, as I believed that was where her mum was from and had returned to. I would have no way of finding her up there, so I had to live this in God's hands.

2010: Can I Continue Living?

Eleven years have passed, and still, every January, thoughts of Sheldon's passing seized my thinking as I relieved the memory and feeling of pain. I tried to calm myself, but it felt like an emotional hell.

One day, I woke up feeling so fed up with waking up tired and pained. I asked myself what I felt Sheldon would say if he could talk to me about what he had been observing. I got a clear answer.

I am still his mum.

I know he very much enjoyed the time he spent with me. I spent so much time asking questions about how, why, and where he had died instead of recalling the joys we experienced together. '*Sorry Sheldon*'. I know he would not want me to allow our great times to be erased by this. Moving forward, I would not allow your physical absence to prevent things from happening that you would have treasured.

This was my second major decision.

2012

I got a call from my daughter, Sherry. A lady had contacted her claiming that she had been caring for Candace in London, no less than a ten-minute walk from where we used to live. So, while I walked around that community, asking God to keep her safe wherever she was, she was possibly one of the children I passed by.

Thankfully, her carer was as keen as I was to introduce us. The journey to connecting with this once-lost grand-child had begun.

She had found us. God kept her safe. She was closer than we realised. More questions.

How had this lady found us? Is this how we experience miracles?

Yes, I have consistently prayed for this child, not knowing where or how she was faring but was God really paying attention to me? Even through my angry railing at Him?

How often do we reflect on how God feels about us personally? Do we really feel that we deserve or ever get special, individualised attention from Him? We hear that God gave His Son because He loves us, but what is our personal experience of what this means, especially when we experience great suffering?

Do we notice anything or feel the need to be grateful for anything while sinking in extreme pain from loss, fear, or disappointment?

Finding Candace felt like seeing God's work first-hand in my life. I could feel her dad's smile.

2015

My husband, Rev. Ron Nathan and I are given the opportunity to lead The Freedom Church (AME Zion) in London. This was a big surprise, considering our plans for Trinidad, but we embraced it. I wondered if Sheldon's children would come to worship with us. As I was initially one of Jehovah's Witnesses, Sheldon spent his early years going to a Kingdom Hall with myself and his great grandmother, who he adored. It wasn't a cool image to identify as a churchgoer or a believer in his environment, but Sheldon carried his love for God in his heart. Those that experienced him outside the constraints of his young adult environment knew this about him. He would be so pleased knowing that his children would have an opportunity to build a relationship with God.

One big challenge lay ahead though: these were not little children who could be brought to church; they needed to be consulted with. Did I feel up to it? It felt more important that I tried to build a warm relationship with each of them. Despite my efforts, we had already been seriously challenged in doing this. I had to trust that God could use other means to attract them to Him if that were to be.

All three of Sheldon's children had been taught about God and taken to a place of worship through their upbringing, but none of them would call themselves followers of Jesus Christ. During the four years that followed, they visited on a couple of special occasions, but they politely let me know that they weren't really believers. This was unsurprising, given their experience. Even I, who believed strongly before losing Sheldon, only narrowly held onto my faith after his passing.

What would God have me do at this time? God had clearly demonstrated His intention to care for my needs, so what was He going to do for and with my seven grandchildren at this time? I will continue to pray, even when it feels difficult to trust. The quote from Psalm 46:10: '*be still and know that I am God...*' lives in my soul.

2019

The year is coming to an end, and we are asked to take up a post in Barbados—yeah!! This was an answer to our prayer for Ron to be closer to his parents. Well, operation-worship-with-my-grandchildren didn't work; '*sorry Sheldon*'. Your children are now grown and didn't feel they believed or wanted to live as a believer. My response to them as it was for you was to respect their spiritual decision. My decision would be to continue praying for them while asking God what He would have me do.

2020—Speak God; Your Servant Is Listening

As the year gets started, a terror named COVID-19 enters our world. We get an opportunity to visit Ron's parents for seven days before the borders of Trinidad & Tobago are closed. How thankful I am to be married to a clear-thinking prophet in this season.

My husband, Ronald Nathan, landed in Barbados in March to take up his new post at Hoggard AME Zion church. I was unable to join him. Now, more than ever, I felt I needed God to guide me.

I longed to see my grandchildren. Sherry seemed to be managing with her children, and Sheldon's son, along with his other daughter, lived with friends and family. But I was particularly concerned about Candace, who now lived alone since graduating from university. I wondered how she was coping during the lockdown. I couldn't talk with her as often as I liked.

By the summer, I managed to spend a few days with Candace. Chats with her have felt like a gift.

We had conversations about how the church has sometimes poorly handled the Bible. We all start as sinners, but some Christians forget how it felt when they didn't believe. Even if those who converted remembered how it felt as a newcomer, it may help congregations to be more caring in their interactions with seekers and newcomers to the spiritual family.

July arrived, and an opportunity presented itself, and I finally got to leave the UK to join Ron in our new territory. Candace felt that she had only just started building a relationship with us and wanted to follow, not yet ready to let us go.

So much is unfamiliar and uncertain at this time; why not let her come? Mental well-being is one of the top priorities we are warned about as social and physical isolation takes its toll on societies. How challenging it is to be taking up new responsibilities in a new country during a global crisis! By now, I had understood that when things look impossible, hand them over to God.

These days of COVID-19-induced-terror, many have fallen into states of depression and suicidal ideation. To feel inner peace at this time is truly a blessing. What can be done while churches and their leaders are in lockdown? He responded that I should make myself available to nurture the development of a relationship between Him (God) and Candace. I could think of nothing else more reliable to leave any of my grandchildren with. These days remind us that none of us can know or have control over when we will die.

During this time of encouraging Candace's investigation of God, she in return encouraged me to offer guidance in a supportive place that my other biological grandchildren could access. I also offered help to other young people who did not have access to advice from their grandparents or elders.

This gave birth to an Instagram engagement called @ChattingWithGranma, where I reach out to virtual grandchildren via weekly videos and sharing insights from an elder's perspective. I have also committed to a weekly Clubhouse discussion where people can come to think, reason, and share opinions with Granma Glynis around their interests or dilemmas.

The human is a social animal created for interactions, so isolation is one of the worst conditions it can endure. My digital activities to facilitate social interaction, even during physical distancing rules, contribute to helping people navigate these times.

Another reminder through this intergenerational exchange has been that mindset is everything. If we have programmed ourselves or have been programmed via culture to think and behave in a certain way, it becomes our normal (default) through all our experiences. Therefore, it seems that it takes an active decision followed by intentional behaviour to truly connect ourselves to God's will. God gave us free will, so we are allowed to choose our way forward.

Our life experiences and culture can obscure a clear vision of the process of aligning our actions with God's will, and our emotions can present themselves as a credible reason to override thoughtful decision-making. Nevertheless, when we are able to choose God, we inadvertently choose to engage His grace and guidance. God's grace is sufficient to perform difficult human activities—those which we call miracles.

During a five-month sabbatical from her normal routine, Candace allowed herself to question and challenge all angles of her disbelief about God. In the embrace of a caring group of people in the Hoggard AME Zion church, her sincere and healthy desire to embrace truth found

God waiting to navigate her via a process that culminated in her choosing to accept Jesus Christ as her personal saviour.

Our family reflection on this five-month period is that it is indeed a miracle—*From Disbelief to Acceptance*. Observing her transformation felt similar to watching my journey of reframing the loss of my son's physical presence. The loss of Sheldon acted as a catalyst for the miracle of Candace finding the route to abundant life. In navigating my experience, I had to make many decisions, the first being to hand the outcome over to God, but these decisions couldn't be made until I was emotionally able.

What miracle would you like to see unfold on your life journey? When you are ready to choose, I suspect that Psalms 46:10, "...be still and know that I am God..." may be helpful to your journey through whatever the challenges.

I wish you peace and love as you navigate your journey.

10

HOW PAIN GAVE WAY TO NEW LIFE AND NEW VENTURES: NAVIGATING SUFFERING TO SUCCESS

SHIREEN MORRISON

Will my unborn child die?

Will I go to heaven?

Will I have to choose between my baby's life and mine?

These were all the questions that entered my head whilst my husband and I embraced at a very busy hospital corridor. I remember feeling like I was in a nasty soap opera episode as blurred colours whizzed by. I looked at Andrew's face, and I could see the genuine love he had for me. Helpless and vulnerable, I reflected in the abandoned wheelchair we found in the hallway after my legs no longer allowed me to walk.

Two months before that day, I had experienced severe pain in my legs, night after night. A kind of dead-like feeling; my legs were so painful to move or simply roll over. I had to grab the covers and pull myself around to find a comfortable position. As I was coming to the end of my fourth pregnancy, I believed this could be normal, but occasionally, I would be in so much pain that I would call my mum to discuss *'is this normal in pregnancy'*? Some nights got really bad that I would call triage, but only to be advised that it was normal in pregnancy to get a tummy belt. I was instructed to have some pain killers, and I would be fine, as symphysis pubis dysfunction (SPD) was inevitable during the third trimester.

Symphysis pubis dysfunction even sounded scary, but they never referred to it as that. It was "SPD", and I had no clue what it was. Having had three previous babies, you would think I would be an 'expert', but I assured myself that every pregnancy is different, and no question is ever a silly one.

Although things became difficult, I continued my daily routines, taking my three other children to school, cleaning, washing the clothes, cooking, and everything seemed to be in slow motion. I had to sit on a stool by the washing machine to take the clothes out, and I constantly questioned if I was okay or whether it was just part of the parcel. I used to beg Andrew, my husband, not to go to work but eventually gave up. I felt like I was just being a needy wife that could not cope. I hadn't acknowledged that my body was unbearable until the morning I got up and cried while dragging myself to the bathroom, and then cried in agony all the way back. This was NOT normal.

Speaking to my mum once again, I explained how life had become so difficult. This time, her response changed.

She said, *"Come to the hospital with me this morning, I have a blood test, and you can check yourself at the same time."* I agreed.

Once at the hospital, the doctors gave me the usual check-up: blood pressure fine, no temperature, all good and then the doctor looked down at my legs. It's funny how not until it was highlighted did I realise the problem was staring me right in the face. One leg was extremely bigger than the other, to the point where I wondered why this was not apparent to me all along. But what did this mean? I didn't know until the doctor came to see me.

It was not long until Andrew was called to the hospital. The doctor arranged a scan to investigate the size difference of my legs further. Pondering on this now, I did not think the outcome would have been so devastating.

The young man doing the scan seemed quite upbeat when conducting the examination, like nothing phased him. I was getting the whole been there, done it, and got the T-shirt sort of vibe about him. However, the results showed that I had a blood clot in my leg but not just any blood clot. It was humongous. The doctors were astounded. No medical professional could believe that a blood clot that size had gone unnoticed for that length of time. They were surprised the clot had not broken into pieces, circulated around my body, and started to affect other organs. Eagerly, medical students gathered around and asked me the same questions the doctors had. They all started to sound like an echo.

Being quite a healthy individual with no health-related issues, it was hard to come around to the idea that I had deep vein thrombosis (DVT) in pregnancy. I was high risk, and all that stood between me and death was my body cooperating with the blood thinners administered twice a day for treatment. Andrew began steering the home-life ship, and my mother-in-law moved in for a couple of weeks.

At the altar, only a few months before, I empathised with a fellow church member at the thought of having a medical problem that affected their everyday activities. I was so grateful that it was not me undertaking the stresses and implications, but now, it was me in the similar situation. It hurt to stand up; it hurt to sit down, and I had to take a backseat in my life.

I was on crutches and had to take injections twice a day. I hate medication, so this was my worst nightmare. I couldn't give myself the injections, and eventually, I started to believe Andrew was enjoying injecting me!! Every time I had to take the injection, I began feeling anxious, and when I finally received the Fragmin, the burning sensation radiated throughout my whole body.

The doctors had a health plan and decided within a week, I'd be induced; no question. Being my first time of getting induced, I had no clue what to expect. Receiving the drip meant that the labour pains came thick and fast. At the peak of the labour pains, I sat on the bed, screaming for the pain to stop. The student doctors were back, scribbling away on their notebooks. Fascinated and asking more questions: *"Have you ever had a blood clot before?"*

"No!" Scribble, scribble, scribble.

"Has anyone in your family had a blood clot before?"

"No! Oooohhhh, aaaahhhh" scribble, scribble, scribble.

All I wanted to say to them was, *'Can't you see I am in labour here and not just a science experiment'!'*

Home

Returning home with my newborn, Jeremiah-James, was a challenging time. I continued in pain and had to attend the hospital regularly. I had to take warfarin for three months after the pregnancy to ensure my blood levels were restored. After a month on paternity leave, Andrew went back to work, and I was back to the normal mother and wife duties. I had to think fast. I called the school and explained to them what had happened, and they allowed me to drop and collect my then eight- and three-year-old from the school reception so I wouldn't have to walk around the entire playground during the school run. They also let me park in the school car park. Thank God for the little blessings. I even remember a teacher holding my newborn as I loaded everybody into the car. Once home, the hours seemed incredibly long, waiting for Andrew to return home.

Tensions were high at home as every day rolled into another. Andrew and I were approaching almost four years of marriage, and we had four children, all under the age of ten. Someone mentioned that with that kind of story, I could write a book. When would I have time to write a book!!? Andrew was dealing with the bereavement of his beloved father. Just before I found out I was pregnant, Dad passed on. Life can seem so unbearable at times.

Sometimes, I would go in the car and scream and break down and plead for God to help me through. On my birthday, after Jeremiah was born, Andrew couldn't take any more time off work, and I remember sitting down, crying because all I wanted to do was have a shower on my birthday. My sisters rescued me and brought me a fry up from a local café, and I was able to get dressed and relax for a few hours. Absolute bliss.

I began resenting Andrew's job and how hands-on he seemed to be at work but when he returned home, he was burnt out. I used to hate speaking to him on his lunch break to hear how stress-free he sounded, but yet, I felt like I was struggling with no time for myself. Fridays were the worst, or when he had a social event at the company and would return after dinner, only having moments before the kid's bedtime. The house looked chaotic every time I turned around.

Renewed Passion

I wanted more than this for my children, my marriage, and myself. I needed more. I started looking around me for things to reignite my passion and bring back some of my joy. I'm a social person, and I've always loved going out. I was reminded of when I had realised the minimal opportunities and events for Christians to enjoy themselves except for church services and conventions. I believed as young Christians, God wanted people to live life to the fullest and enjoy time together. So, though new in our relationship, Andrew and I started organising banqueting events with live music. This seemed successful, and there was a great buzz around the events we put on. However, after the third event, I gave birth to my second child, then two children followed with small gaps in-between. I was officially a housewife, and all that seemed so far from where I had found myself. I had to get back to that.

I started to help organise concerts and fashion shows for my church and often hire out the décor that I had from the banqueting events I used to organise.

After attending a business course organised by the Pentecostal credit union and hosted by Claudine and Patrick Reid, we realised the opportunity to start our own décor hire company. The common interest ignited a passion within us once again. The double workshops during the week meant that my husband and I got to go out—just us. We got to make friends and meet like-minded people. We got to discuss our passion and dreams and saw them form before our eyes. We spent the hour drive there and back, rekindling that spark we had all those years ago. He saw me, and I saw him.

As life happens, things got harder. We were told to leave our house because the landlord wanted to sell it. We didn't know what to do, so we decided to move in with my mum, and this had some challenges too. After two years of organising our finances, we found a house to rent. We had to completely reposition ourselves and decide what we wanted for our future. What did we want for our future? Andrew had previous experience within the mainstream music industry, and he wanted to create a platform for the Christian Community. Visions TV Online was birthed after God urged Andrew to follow his passion. It was time to step out in faith!!

We began putting ourselves out on a limb. Wherever there was an event in the gospel/Christian community, we were there. Premier Gospel Awards, Integrity Studio in Brighton, and Big Church Day out, to name a few amazing events. Within two years, Visions TV Online allowed us to interview Donnie McClurkin, get invited to his 60th birthday party in New York, and be the first UK Media representatives for the Stellar Awards. We were able to attend important meetings hosted by astepfwd and 7Gospeltracks to help pan out the structure and impact of The GMIA. Wow! God is so so good!

During the pandemic, we had faith in God for multiple things—to deliver our daughter safely into the world, even after my complications with baby number four. I was trusting that baby number five would arrive safe and sound, and she did!! Having a baby throughout lockdown was a very surreal experience, but that's a story for another day! We had many lessons of trusting God to provide for us, which was highlighted when Andrew took the plunge to resign from his full-time job. As soon as Andrew stepped out, the lockdown came into place.

However, God continued to provide, and we never lacked. The exact money that was needed came at the right time to be able to commit to the purchase. God created an opportunity to buy another company, and UnboundPR arose. Having the businesses allowed Andrew and I to find our common interests again and helped us work together as Bosses to a partnership of two businesses. It enabled us to use skills that we didn't even know that we had. I became the presenter and worked tirelessly in the background, conducting emails and liaising with Artists. Andrew would work hard with his technical skills, filming, editing, and creating visual events.

Although life has been very hard at times, God has always been faithful, and He was always there. God has seen us at our worst, and He has seen us at our best, and He says that we are "fearfully and wonderfully made". Therefore, there are no mistakes where He is concerned. God has always provided for us, even when we felt like we were hanging by a thread and there was no way. He certainly made a way. We are forever grateful.

What will my children remember about me? Will they be proud to have a mother like me? How am I helping them be the best version of themselves? Staring in awe at our five children, these questions spring to mind. Knowing that I love them and would do anything for them reassures me that I will always try to be the best mum I can be, and Andrew will always be the father that the children will be proud of.

From us, I hope they glean an understanding that we pushed the boundaries, that we were determined and worked hard to lay a foundation for them. All while ensuring that we were present at home, watching them grow, and showing them a love that knows no bounds. That surely, is our legacy.

11

WOMAN OF FAITH: NAVIGATING AUTHENTICITY

ANIKA-ADÉL BARNES

As I sit here thinking about what to write and share with the potential recipient of these words, the first thing that hits me is absolute dread and fear.

What if I can't cope with the responses I get back? I don't want to be trolled. Once I write this, it's out there. It is no longer hidden deep within me. I feel like I'm dying to know but afraid to find out. Somewhere between wanting to know, can I actually write something that will one day be published? Will my experience of navigating this season of my life resonate with anyone else out there? Should this short excerpt of one of many challenging chapters in my life help another meandering soul, even just one, then I suppose feeling the anxiety and trepidation that I'm having at this moment may be worth it. On the other hand, wanting to hide away, stay mute, invulnerable, and pour the depths of myself out over these coming pages and not let anyone have a glimpse into my internal space are similarly alluring.

I sit here in my spare room with a baby pink mechanical pencil in hand, along with my luxurious writing pad, with beautiful rose gold, grey, marble metallic print in the other hand. Poised, I take a deep breath and whisper to myself in the words of bestselling author Susan Jeffers, 'Feel the fear and do it anyway'.

It was 15th February 2020; I sat in my living room with my friend. I can't remember what was on the television. In fact, if memory serves me correctly, we were both physically present in the room but mentally absent. I was on one sofa scrolling away on my iPad, and they were on the two-seater engrossed in something on their device. It was one of those lazy Sundays.

My friend looks up and says, *'Oh, Caroline Flack is dead'*. Immediately, I took to Twitter (at that time, that was the only social media platform I was signed up to). I read beautiful tributes and comments from Caroline's family, friends, acquaintances, and the general public. Everyone was expressing their condolences and sadness.

For those who may not be familiar with Caroline Flack, she was an English television and radio presenter who worked on *I'm A Celebrity...Get Me Out Of Here*, *The Xtra Factor*, and *Love Island*. Whilst I did not particularly follow Caroline's career, I did admire what appeared to me to be a young vibrant woman living her best life and not conforming to all the societal norms. Maybe because I felt there was something relatable about her lifestyle.

My feelings were a mixture of sorrow, shock, upset, and a deep sense of sadness and regret that Caroline's precious life had come to such a tragic end. But my strongest emotion and perhaps the most startling emotion I was experiencing was that I felt jealous.

I'm sure those who know me and others who don't but are reading this may be thinking, *why would you be jealous of a woman who has died*? And more concerningly, a woman who must have been in a very dark, lonely, sad, and scary place to have taken her own life.

Well, the truth is, or at least, it was at that time I was jealous that she had the guts, the audacity, and the bravery to go through with it.

However, my feelings of envy for such a heart-breaking event would lead my emotions to turn to guilt, self-loathing, and shame. I would question myself, *'Why can't I sustain any form of contentment? Why can't I fix myself? What's wrong with me? Am I that broken? Why am I so sad?'* I would search my soul for the answers and only get myself in a worse state as I did not have the tools to mend myself. I remember a few years back when I was at a crossroad in my career, and I went for a course in Careers Counselling. The Career Advisor frowned and looked at me over the top of the lenses of her glasses and said, *'Hmm...healer can't heal thyself'*. This statement has always stayed with me.

Inside, I felt a deep sense of despair and being at a loss. I was miserable and exhausted. Miserable that life wasn't really going to plan, even though I'm not sure I really had a plan other than survival. I was exhausted from keeping up the pretence that I was okay when really I wasn't. I was tired of having to put my work face on, as I would call it, whereby I faked smiles and exchanged superficial pleasantries with those outside of my trusted inner circle.

The following day, I arrived at work still feeling very flat, low, and saddened about Caroline, of course. But equally concerned and disturbed about the thoughts in my own head of not wanting to be here, I walked across the car park and entered my place of work. I smiled, greeted co-workers, and inquired about their welfare and weekends. I also found something agreeable to say in response to what they shared with me. While all the time, a little voice within says, *'Hold it together, girl. Fake it till you make it'.*

I turned on my computer and left the office to head to the ladies to check my reflection in the mirror. I looked into my eyes just to check what story they may tell and the secrets they unknowingly may be emanating. I gave myself a reassuring smile. On route back to my desk, I make a cuppa and then stared at my screen. I typed into Google, 'Therapy Directory' and hit send. The website then asked me to state my locality and provided a list of a few hundred professionals in my area. This was not the first time I had spoken to a counsellor. I've always been a big advocate for seeking help and support when dealing with life challenges. My gauge is, if I'm struggling to move through an issue, no matter how small or big it is, then it is time to seek help. However, I will say that I don't like going through the therapy process because it is hard. It is painful my mind has to go to places that I would not want to return to, the things I would rather brush under that big old dusty metaphorical carpet. Therapy is a strange process. I still feel the intensity of the emotions that have already been lived through, sometimes years after the event occurred. The process does bring its rewards, allowing me to find healing, closure, or mere acceptance of what has been. I have also realised that revisiting my former experiences and versions of myself has allowed me to adjust my behaviour and let go of things, patterns, or habits that no longer serve or enable me to become a whole version of myself. I like to say that I'm an updated operating system, a bit like an Apple device, each time upgrading to version AAB 1.1, AAB 1.2, AAB. 1.25, etc., and becoming more effective at doing life and looking after oneself.

I contacted a few therapists whose profiles had a picture. I intentionally reached out to those women who were of a Black or Minority background. It was not because I felt that a therapist of White ethnic origin would not be equally as professional and good at their craft as a person of colour. I just felt that I needed to speak to someone who has lived out some experiences of the challenges that people of colour go through daily. For me to be truly open and honest in telling my truth and bringing my whole self into the room, and getting the most out of therapy, I felt I needed to sit opposite someone who shares some similarities to me as a Black woman.

There! I had made my decision. I closed the page and got on with the rest of my working day.

After work, I walked back across the car park, got into my car, sat there for five minutes or so, recollecting myself. When I arrived home, I thanked God that I survived the day.

The following Thursday, I rang the doorbell. A small petite lady I assumed was of Eastern Asian origin answered the door and welcomed me into her home and workspace. She had welcoming eyes and a warm smile. I told her that I was fed up with being fed up, and I just couldn't make myself happy. I explained that this was a feeling that had been with me for some time (I couldn't admit to her that I was having suicidal thoughts and that I did not want to be alive, which felt like bearing my soul a bit too intimately). But I did tell her the mental anguish and torment that I faced and that every day was literally a battle to drag myself through.

I've always been fascinated by the topic of mental health and what makes us happy, or at very least, at peace and in a place of contentment from both a psychological view and other perspectives such as religion/spirituality. Why? Because I've always felt a bizarre sense of despair, loneliness, and not belonging here, in the world I mean—not wanting to be here, alive. I've often questioned whether I was born with some hormonal deficits that made me more predisposed to being sad and feeling this to such a great extent that it feels debilitating. When I have read about depression, it is often suggested that there is a shortfall or imbalance of certain chemicals within the brain, whilst other research suggests genetic vulnerability. From my experience, I believe that I am one of those people who has to constantly train my mind to think in a helpful way and not have toxic invasive thoughts of beating myself up or putting myself down and seeing things from a pessimistic perspective. In contrast, when at work or speaking to others in need, I can be hopeful and positive that their circumstances could change and improve, offering them support and encouragement.

So, I began the internal work once again, but this time, I was a little more determined than previous attempts to try and find my inner peace.

Each Thursday evening, I met my therapist. At the beginning of my life, we started speaking about childhood, adolescence, relationships, traumatic life events, health, work, and everything in-between. We delved a little deeper into some areas more than others. However, I could not pinpoint any one event or experience that had brought me to where I was internally. Instead, I probably identified a series of things stemming from all the key areas of life that had led me to feel this way.

A few weeks after commencing my therapeutic journey, the United Kingdom was thrown into a national lockdown in response to the global COVID-19 pandemic. The first few weeks were extremely challenging, and my anxiety was very high, as were most peoples at this time. Once I got into the flow of my new normal (i.e., being alone every day, working from home, and going out for an hour a day), I told myself I would use this time as an opportunity to really explore my mind and face myself. This time gave me the chance to exhale as I often felt like I was walking around in a state of holding my breath whilst trying to keep myself together.

I constructed myself a different daily routine as I felt that I needed some structure to my new daily format. Now, there was all this spare time not having to do a long commute on the motorway. This consisted of starting my morning with some physical activities. I am so not a natural morning person and really don't feel alive until around 11 a.m., but the movement allowed my mind and body to fully wake up and start my day in a controlled manner. I also valued that I had invested in my wellbeing at the start of the day before the demands of Microsoft Teams would require my attention. I also ensured that I read something positive following this, which was usually a daily devotional on the Bible app and the verse of the day. I would then shower and get on with my working day. After work, I went out for my hour's walk that Prime Minister Boris Johnson had instructed that we do, occasionally sneaking in an extra 20 minutes for medicinal purposes, of course. Often, during these walks, I would spend time speaking to God in prayer. I poured my heart out to my Creator and prayed for all those dealing with the pandemic in their various capacities worldwide. And just before bed, I would write in my gratitude journal five things to be thankful for, or at least, I ought to be thankful for.

My approach to looking after my mental health became a very much holistic one, which I tackled from a mind, body, and spirit angle. I knew talking therapies such as Cognitive Behaviour Therapy was a method to address thought patterns, whilst lots of research also suggests looking at diet to enhance mood. Being a woman of faith, I spent time reading bible scriptures about the mind, specifically making these my daily affirmations. Whenever I had an unhelpful thought, or my mind was going down a rabbit hole of negativity, I would say to myself, 'Take every thought captive and make it obedient to the word of God' *(2 Corinthians 10:5)* or '*For God has not given me a spirit of fear, but of power and of love and of a sound mind'*, (2 Timothy 1:7).

I would repeat these, and soon enough, I had forgotten whatever it was that had crept into my head. I memorised as many scriptures that I could, where the Bible referenced the mind and our thoughts. I felt that if I had these in my arsenal, I could battle with my mind.

I also spent time looking at what I was feeding my mind. I believe that a diet is not only what we eat but what we consume via television, social media, conversations with others, etc. So, I became very intentional about this area. I've always been one to monitor what I watch on TV, ensuring that I don't watch too much News. I particularly avoid the News at 10 p.m., even more so throughout the pandemic, as I did not want my mind to be on anything that may upset me or increase my anxiety before going to sleep. But I do love a good crime drama or true crime documentary, which I think is due to my work. However, I ensured that I would also indulge in things full of positivity and personal development. So, I would often listen to a sermon, health podcast, or motivational speech whilst doing chores or when I'm out on my daily walks. At the end of October 2020, I opted in for a surgical procedure at a hospital. When I was discharged, I spent my sick leave watching comedies, just allowing myself to have a good old giggle. I thought to myself; I'm sure laughter would help me heal a little faster. Whether it did or not, I'm not entirely sure, but it stopped me from sitting around and feeling sorry for myself. It debarred me from focusing on the physical and psychological pain of healing, and it was a good distraction technique.

As I reflect on the past 12 months, I discovered the beauty in the ordinary - watching the seasons change, kicking autumn leaves, jumping in puddles in the rain and getting covered in mud, taking pictures of a frozen winter's lake, seeing the first daffodils of spring, and reading a book in a park on a summer's day. This taught me that just like the seasons change, I evolve both internally and my external circumstances change too. I have learnt to hang on, not to give up. I have learnt that healing is a process and one that takes as long as it takes. I also learnt the fragility of life in a year filled with so much tragedy around the globe captured in the media where many were fighting to be alive on ventilators, and some unwillingly lost their lives whilst innocent others were killed by the very authorities that should have kept them safe. Ohh, I so realised what a gift it is to be alive.

Whatever this next season of my life shall unfold, my hope is that *'and still I shall rise'* (Maya Angelou). Surely, living life to the full means having an assortment of experiences and feeling the entire spectrum of emotions - from the bliss to the mundane, despair and all that lies between.

12

FROM PAIN TO PURPOSE: NAVIGATING MISCARRIAGE AND CHURCH HURTS

DENISE H LAWRENCE

"Ask, and you will receive; seek, and you will find. Knock, and the door will be open for you" **(Mathew 7:7; GNT).**

As I stood before 350 congregants amid the sanctuary, I was asked by the visiting Preacher to share the desires of my heart. I shared that I desired to grow more in the Lord. He said, *"That's great; God is going to use you mightily. You are a dynamic and powerful intercessor and preacher. You will operate highly in the gifts of the prophetic and teachings, but that's not only it now."* Satisfied with those words of confirmation, I turned slightly to the left to return to my seat. In that split second, the Preacher commanded me to stop, and I did. Then the Prophet continued to speak to me, and I was blown away as these words escaped his parted lips, "*God said, go forth; He is the one. It is your time, and you shall have.*" The reassurance of God's prophetic words resonated with me; at that moment, I was transfixed. My spirit rejoiced with volcanic worship that demolished the foundations of doubt, fear, insecurity, and spiritual bondage. I heard the whispers and chatters; I saw the facial expressions of surprise and confusion while others nodded in agreement. I rushed home with the intention of not allowing anything to disrupt the prophetic declaration.

Soon after, in the warm summer of July 2010, I married my husband George, with our two children Kayla and Junior, from my previous marriage, along with family and friends by our side. We exchanged our vows on the beach, with our feet in the sand on the beautiful island of Jamaica. George resided in Jamaica, so we agreed to alternate travel plans between Jamaica and the United States until we decided where home would be for our new family. The following year, in the summer of 2011, what should have been a regular two to three months' vacation for our family, turned out to be the rollercoaster test of my faith, the prophetic word, and the sanity of my mind. After church on Sunday, then dinner by George's aunt, our family was filled with glee, but the events at midday on Monday, July 22nd, changed my life trajectory.

There I was, alone, in a space wreaked with despair as worries lingered despite how often the squeaky glass doors opened. Everyone sat, wondering who would be next, based on how the nurses and doctors viewed life's priority; yet ironically, I was losing a life. The warm blood sliding slowly alongside my wobbly legs, possibly staining the hard and uncomfortable orange monobloc chairs, and my eyes constantly staring down at my weak tapping feet. My fingers were piercing inside each palm, alternating with twists and knots, as if somehow it would sedate the internal emotional turmoil.

Was this my reality? This space and current happenings were not the picturesque three-month summer vacation in the beautiful Jamaican paradise we planned. I don't recall signing an agreement to end up at St. Ann's Bay Hospital on Seville Road, having a miscarriage. How did I get here? Was this the honest answer to my prayers: "*God give me the desires of my heart, be it your perfect will for me to remarry, ensure that, oh, also don't forget this, and yeah bless my womb?*" I'm sorry, I checked, and "miscarriage" is not found in the word *search*. Yes, there are two children from my previous marriage, but George has none, and I am now age 40. Something went wrong. The prophetic word was "*God said...you will have*", but now this! Okay, will someone please rewind and pause the movie?

Scared, hesitant, embarrassed, and repelled at the hospital's condition and the treatment I received, I sat there for two more hours and bled, seething with anger. With soaked garments, I dragged myself up the hill to the ward they assigned me. Upon entering, I questioned if I was in the right place. I approached the desk, and the nurse said, in the Jamaican vernacular, '*Miss, I beg u, lay dung right ova deh so*' (Ma'am, would you please go to my right and lay on the bed?) "Here?" I asked, pointing to her right. '*Yes, right deh so, dat bed inna di middle*' (Yes, exactly there, the middle bed specifically). So, I placed my ultimately failed body upon '*that bed*' in the middle.

I felt alone amidst a sea of women; a few were elderly patients, others as young as mid-twenties, with different sicknesses. I scanned the room, assessing their indisposition, for a sense of assurance that I was in the wrong place. Why am I here? Shouldn't I be in another area, a room where someone can actually 'save' my baby? My baby must be saved; after all, God's word promises that if asked, I shall receive. God will answer my prayers; I kept telling myself. *For everyone that asketh receiveth; and he that seeketh findeth, and to him that knocketh it shall be opened* (Matthew 7:8; KJV). What benefit, purpose, or lesson could come out of me losing my child? I waited for George to arrive.

"Hon, I'm here." It was my husband, George. His voice was comforting while he stuttered, "Everything is going to be all right." It was not Bob Marley; it was my husband. So yeah, everything would be all right. With silent tears running down my face, my heart sank in my chest, and I exhaled in his arms. But like a drowning victim underwater, I did not aspirate, as the rude, loud, and obnoxious nurse said, "*Sha u hafi come out, you no fi deh in yah so, a jus woman fi in yah*" (Sir, I'm afraid you must leave; men are not allowed in here. This is a woman's unit only). Not having him by my bedside, at that moment, another life died. Call a code blue because my 'hope' just died of cardiac arrest. George scoped and securely held my defeated body and drowned spirit, and we went outside on the corridors.

After much time, I reluctantly re-entered the room and laid on '*that bed*'—unaware of how the strategic positioning of '*that bed*' below the window would play out later. Sometimes amid pain and suffering, we cannot see the blessings of God because we are so fixated on the intensity of the pain. We become blinded to the magnitude of the benefits. That opened window was the portal to our conversations, connections, soul, emotions, and support. *Be thankful in all circumstances, for this is God's will for you who belong to Christ Jesus* (1 Thessalonians 5:18). We held each other's hands for two hours, occasionally letting go for bathroom breaks, then back to the same position. For another hour, non-verbally, we communicated; we shared our fears, agony, despair, hope, resentment, failure, disappointment, and possibly blame. As time drew closer to the end of visiting hours, we both gasped for air buried so deep beneath the whys, hows, and whats. As he slowly let go of my trembling, cold hands, it was apparent that life, hope, and faith were now like a withered maple leaf dancing lifelessly in the wind with no self-agency and inner strength.

This unexpected, unimaginable suffering robbed me of so much. As the night went by, things got darker. As a light sleeper, I overheard the staff pacing the floors, updating charts, and sharing talks with the night crew. "*We are watching her closely; she is bleeding far more than usual; we have changed her bedding twice already,*" one nurse said. Then I heard her say, "*Yeah, you guys, see, look,*" (view guys) while not graciously pulling the covers off my leg, to show the world the pool of blood beneath me. "*Yeah, wi ha fi watch har so shi no bleed to death, mi dear,*" (She must be watched closely, as we are concerned she will bleed to death). That distinct unwelcoming voice was the last thing I heard.

With no will to live, I didn't flinch, and that sentence, of possibly bleeding to death, was the lullaby to which I fell asleep. Just before I completely closed my eyes, I remembered the scripture, *"Death and life are in the power of the tongue: and they that love it shall eat the fruit thereof"* (Proverbs 18:21; KJV). With the bit of remaining strength I had, I whispered to God, *"I will not die but live, and will proclaim what...the LORD has done. I shall not die, but live, and declare the works of the LORD* (Psalm 118:17; KJV). Pain is a distraction, but no matter how severe or how dark things may appear, even when death is lingering, use the scriptures to speak hope, victory, and life. Six hours later, but what felt like five minutes to me, I heard piercing screams and loud noises, and I arose only to question if I was having a nightmare. I rubbed my eyes twice for a sense of reality. I saw men, women, and white sheets tossed over two bodies and empty spaces on my right and my left. What was happening? The sting of death came in. The older woman on my left and the youngster on my right died during the night. I remained paralyzed, numb, pinned to *'that bed'* like a patient strapped in a psychiatric ward. Stunned, I was unable to process the grace of God over my life, even at that moment.

On Wednesday, August 24th, close to noon, with the approval letter from R.H, Consultant, Obstetrics, and Gynecology, which read, *"the above-named patient was pregnant and has had a complete miscarriage."* Though my child died, I was alive. Death was spoken, but the power of God within me said life: *"And all things, whatsoever ye shall ask in prayer, believing, ye shall receive"* (Mathew 21:22; KJV). The whispers from my lips were the prayers of my heart. I prayed for life. Sometimes, while enduring pain, it is hard to see a purpose, especially if what you were trusting God for is not evident, when the prayers seem unanswered. One of the devil's strategies is deceiving believers to make us doubt God's faithfulness in answering our prayers. The *'father of lies'* would have us believe that God's ear somehow is shut to our cries. The truth is that our prayers are answered. The answers we receive are not the ones we likely expected, but they are just the same. What are your challenges today? Are you in a state of grief, dealing with the stings of pain? Are you grieving in hope, suffering in hope, wrestling, struggling, and crying in hope? May I encourage you, even through tears, whisper a prayer; tell the Lord that you trust Him despite the rugged road of life He asks you to walk. At this very moment, begin to praise Him, for growing your faith, for life, and your answered prayers. There is a purpose in your pain: *"Many are the afflictions of the righteous: but the LORD delivereth him out of them all,"* (Psalms 34:19; KJV). The remaining portions of the letter from the Gynecologist read, "*...and she is fit for international travel,*" and I was released. Within a few days, sooner than I wanted, my husband accompanied the children and me to the airport. There we said goodbye to him and boarded the plane back to Connecticut, USA.

Back Home

Like a never-ending saga, upon arrival, I was greeted by my youngest sister with a box of two months' mail along with a rolled-up paper, perplexed as to why it was not in the enclosed box. I quickly checked. In my hands, a summons for the court stated that the Ex was petitioning for custody agreements and child support, which ironically, he defaulted on in the last five years. What in the Texas tornado is going on here!? I passed out.

Now listen, I have experienced many trials, struggles, abuse, abandonment, rejection, and a myriad of heartaches; however, for this one right here, right now, I had no language. Throughout this Christian journey, there will be circumstances, situations, and tragedies that will rip our hearts. Pain can crack the foundations of our faith. However, we must not allow it. Do not allow your story to end there. I know what living with pain is; this story is only a few lines to my life, which God continues to write. Your account doesn't end here; remember that His resurrecting power is on the way. There is purpose in your pain. "Haven't *I commanded thee? Be strong and of a good courage; be not afraid, neither be thou dismayed: for the Lord thy God is with thee whithersoever thou goest*" (Joshua 1:9; KJV).

I went into my living room and fell asleep. A few hours later, I spoke with George over the phone, feeling helpless, hopeless, and isolated, having no one to share his experience with. He later shared that he was also feeling empty at the time. Two people were experiencing pain triggered by the same event but on different levels. Being more robust in faith, I tried to rely on scripture: *"For his anger endureth but a moment; in His favor is life: weeping may endure for a night, but joy cometh in the morning"* (Psalm 30:5; KJV). It was easy to say, but I was uncertain of its reality. After days of licking my wounds, which I dared not share with anyone, I muscled enough strength to contact the lawyer who handled my divorce, but to no avail as he was traveling. While sorting through the mail, I realized that they denied my mortgage modification application. I sat in despair. To add fuel to the already blazing fire, after weeks of isolation and avoiding numerous phone calls, I hesitantly answered, only to hear that someone had shared my personal traumatic experience in the house of worship. Without my permission, my story was shared in a public setting among over two hundred people. My mind raced with angry questions and thoughts: *How did they? Why would they? How could they? The nerve of...!! Who in the world did they think they were? Who gave them the authority?* The gross violation, the pain of betrayal, was brutal. *"For it was not an enemy that reproached me; then I could have borne it: .... But it was thou, a man mine equal, ... We took sweet counsel together and walked unto the house of God in company"* (Psalm 55:12-14; KJV).

The key to overcoming the pain of betrayal is our God-given ability to forgive. *"But I tell you: love your enemies and pray for those who persecute you"* (Mathew 5:44; NIV).

Forgiving 'traitors' can be challenging, but we must find the strength to overcome only through God's Spirit.

This was my story! I had yet to acknowledge and process it. The stigma of miscarriage alone was hard to deal with, and added to that was public humiliation. This abuse of power, poor judgment, and insensitive rhetoric, unbeknownst to me, was the opening of the gate to years of church separation—my personal Isle of Patmos, anxiety, and depression. My cry of grief was magnified stronger than the most significant earthquake sending tremors across the globe. Depression took permanent residency; my sofa became my place of comfort. I lay there, crying for seven days. I could not articulate how I was feeling. I had yet to go through the grief of losing my baby and the future I had imagined. Grief set in.

Navigating grief, brokenness, and betrayal is never easy. The complexity of emotions in grieving, unmet expectations, and unwanted violations feel almost too much to bear. We must allow God to replace our grief with joy. *"And ye now, therefore, have sorrow...and your heart shall rejoice..."* (John 16:22).

Slowly, I was losing touch with reality; occasionally, I was engaged in conversations with my grandmother sitting on the opposite side of the room. What is wrong with that, you may ask? Well, she is deceased. My reactions to miscarriage grew stronger into anger, sadness, and depression. Confusion set in as to what was the cause. Jealousy reared its ugly head at the mere sight of a pregnant woman. Guilt was a winter blanket laying heavily on me. Did I do something wrong? Were there things I could have done differently? The heavy hammer that repeatedly pounded in my mind and heart was that of failure; my body failed me. I failed my marriage and my husband as I could not give him a child. A deep sense of emptiness pulled me further away, and I could no longer trust my body. There was an overwhelming disconnect. Grandma was there; her comforting words and welcoming arms called me. On this particular day, I proceeded towards her, longing to be hugged. As I made my way across the room, the kids unsupervised play got out of control, and they started chasing each other in the house. When Junior bumped into me, the scene played like a mystery movie, and suddenly, grandma disappeared. In a split second, reality returned. I reached for my phone and dialed 211, requested a therapist, counselor, or any professional to help with the state of my mind.

My situation had devolved, and intrusive thoughts and images came to mind over time; compulsive disorders and post-traumatic stress disorder emerged. We know God can do all things, but He also gives us physicians. "*And Jesus answered them, 'Those who are well have no need of a physician, but those who are sick*'" (Luke 5:31; NKJV). Finding comfort in the Bible helps; these verses remind us that God is always with us, no matter what we face. PTSD can affect all areas of a person's life and the lives of their loved ones too. For me, I chose to utilize the combination of secular psychological therapy and biblical insights.

The most challenging part of the journey was the spiritual disconnect. Why God? Where are you? Where is the evidence of the prophetic word? I wrestled within my spirit for the will to rise and trust God for spiritual healing. I had to re-learn the truth of God's word, which reminded me that He would never leave me. I had to pray through my hurt and pain. You may ask, how does one pray while suffering? Well, these are the words that I found: "Lord, I need you..." Our experiences in life, including sorrow, pain, and suffering, equip us in unique ways to have empathy with individuals going through similar situations. It also translates into exhorting, encouraging, and ministering to individuals who share familiar experiences and history. There are many manuals on how to ride a bike, drive a car, or swim. However, I believe if you have never fallen off the bike a few times, narrowly missed an accident or two, or never felt like you were drowning, then your expressions of these things would not be heartfelt, meaningful, or practical to others. Our trials, struggles, successes, failures, pain, and suffering in our lives somehow prepare us to show the love of God. From my pain, God is using me to empower women. "*But I have prayed for thee, that thy faith fails not: and when thou art converted, strengthen thy brethren*" (Luke 22:32; KJV).

Pain has no eyes; therefore, it is blinded to culture, gender, socio-economics, and religious status. Pain is a signal to your spirit that something is trying to get through. I pray that you will not allow the pain to distract you because there is a purpose in your pain. "*My brethren, count it all joy when ye fall...But let patience have her perfect work, that...wanting nothing"* (James 1:2-4; KJV). There is purpose in our pain, talents, and gifts we never knew we had—creativity, inspirational writers, motivational speeches, preaching, encouragers, artists, painters, lyricists, and music. Pain adjusts our attitudes and tests our patience. Pain can be considered an ingredient to the recipe for spiritual growth. Whatever your pain is, allow God to pivot it into purpose.

I Decree and Declare,

- For every struggle in your life, may God accomplish something in your character and spirit.
- Your pain will push you into your promise.
- You are no longer a hostage to your pain.
- Your memories will no longer be filled with pain and torment but with grace and favor.
- You will not become preoccupied with the pain and overlook the promise.

Affirmations

- By His stripes, you are healed (Isaiah 53:5)
- I am assured that all things work for good (Roman 8:28)

Prayer of Salvation

"Whosoever calls on the name of the Lord shall be saved" (Romans 10:13; KJV).

Dear God, I recognize that only through confession of my sins and acknowledging that You raised Jesus from the dead and He is alive today is my path to salvation. I confess my sins and invite you into my life. Thank you for forgiving and accepting me. I am now saved and have eternal life in you.

13

NAVIGATING LIFE WITHOUT HIM

JOSE KALANDA

Until one goes through the reality of losing a close family member it is difficult to understand bereavement and the challenges it brings to life.

Words like sorry for your loss, my condolences, courage and sympathy meant nothing when they were addressed to me. These words become mere empty words that people just say and in the hopes that they make the bereaved feel better or bring comfort. No, real comfort comes with time. In my case, it was brought to me only by the power of the Holy Spirit. As I heard these words of sympathy when I lost my husband, my mind was blank. They meant absolutely nothing to me.

My husband passed away only 20 months after we had relocated to the UK from Africa. We were married for eight years and our daughters were five months old and five years old when we arrived. We had no close family members or friends that I could rely on and the only people I could lean on were my late husband's colleagues.

I remember in 1993 when my close friend lost her husband in Nairobi. She was a newlywed, with no family and no children. On the day of his burial, I saw her sitting on the ground by the graveyard with her eyes fixed on the coffin. She had tears falling down her cheeks and she murmured these words "life is hard, life is very hard". I really felt her pain. As I stood beside her and looked down at her, I thought then that I understood her heartache. But I did not understand the level of pain she was in until it happened to me. Her pain was so bad that a few months later she took her own life. She decided not to challenge life.

My late husband worked for various international organisations. In the eight years of our married life, we moved from country to country. We started our family life in Burundi in Central Africa and we lived there for a year. After this, we moved to Lomé in Togo in West Africa where he secured a new position with another international organisation. He was promoted and was transferred to Nairobi, Kenya in East Africa. After more than three years of living in Nairobi, he got a new job and we moved again. This time we relocated to Addis Ababa in Ethiopia, located in the Horn of Africa. After a while of living in Ethiopia, he was offered a position with an organisation in London.

Life in the UK

We were all excited about this move especially because it was an opportunity to provide the children with some stability in their education. I had visited some European countries before and we had also stayed in America for a short while but this was my first time visiting the United Kingdom. The culture, the lifestyle, and the English accent were really different. I had to adjust but I loved London as soon as we arrived, it was welcoming to me. However, being originally from a French-speaking country I had to learn how to fit in, and to integrate into British society.

I had a fairly good command of the English language already, but I enrolled on an 'English for Speakers of Other Languages' course. I didn't feel alienated having two small children. My older daughter attended an English school in Kenya so she was more or less familiar with the culture. When I enrolled at College to improve my English to a proficient level for use for employment, I also studied basic computer skills, office skills, and did job searches to prepare myself for the job market. I remember one of the college teachers saying this: "The job market is difficult; those with more chances of getting a job are male, white and middle-class". This statement did not deter me from hoping and dreaming that I would find work in the UK.

We arrived in the UK one very cold February morning in 1996. My husband's company had arranged temporary accommodation for us. We secured a school place for our daughter and we were shown around the borough.

In January 1997, my husband started complaining about feeling tired. We didn't really take it seriously because he worked long hours and travelled a lot. However, he became seriously ill in February. In April of the same year, after a number of tests and medical investigations, the dreadful news came and he was diagnosed with an incurable illness. He was in and out of the hospital for medical treatment. He got better and was discharged and came back home in the Summer and was recovering waiting to return to work. Unfortunately, his health deteriorated so rapidly that he was admitted back to the hospital and did not recover.

I went to the hospital every day after dropping my daughter to school. I asked a friend's mother to pick her up from school and I collected her late in the evening. When he got worse, I dropped the children to a family we knew who could keep them overnight. I stayed in the hospital and on that night, he took his last breath and he passed away towards the end of 1997. After I had called his family overseas, I called one of his colleagues to come and pick me up from the hospital and they dropped me home. They stayed with me for a while and then left. Another friend of my husband came that night and stayed with me until the morning.

Navigating Loss

It felt as if I had lost the bones in my body, although I was up and trying to do things, I became like a robot. I went to pick up the children the next morning to return home and as soon as we got home, I tried to explain to them what had happened. I am not sure they understood. The next day I had to go out and start on the funeral arrangements. As I left the house, I remember looking at the sky and not noticing it had lost all its colour. It was November; I did not feel the cold on my skin. I felt numb.

I am grateful to one of my very best friends who was a PhD student in Germany at the time. She arranged to come and stay with me for a few days to help me with the children. In Congo, when someone loses a husband, family and friends stay for a week, or two weeks or even a month to support the bereaved by cooking and cleaning. But this was not the case in the UK. I could not understand why people had to call to arrange a visit during the funeral. In Congo, people don't call or get an invite, they just attend. I struggled to understand this way of life.

Once all the funeral arrangements were completed, I travelled to the Democratic Republic of Congo for the burial. Prayers were being made for me as Congo was a troubled country marred with insecurity, war, and political instability. I thank God for protection during that trip. After the funeral, I remember a friend said this to me: "He is gone. You have small children, think of them and how you will survive with them in this country". I was in pain and hurting, I looked around and I knew that if I continued to remain in the house mourning and doing nothing, my mental health was going to be affected. So, I decided to think about how to occupy my mind.

Finding Life Again

The main priority for me was how to deal with my immigration status to continue to live in the UK. I entered the UK on a four-year dependents work visa because of my husband. As the main claimant was no longer here, I had many unanswered questions: What would be my fate and that of my children? Was my visa valid? Will I be allowed to remain? If yes, how and where do I start? Did I have to return because he was no longer here?

I received two recommendations for a well-established Immigration Lawyer and a Migrant Organisation. I contacted them and they explained the necessary steps I needed to take.

I remember coming across a one-day course on 'Understanding Basic Immigration Control in the UK'. I paid for and attended the course. By the end of it, I became more interested in the subject and wanted to know more. I enrolled in another one-day course relating to immigration. Little did I know that I was at the right place and at the right time as the Training Provider offered a program - a first of its kind to train Community Immigration Advisers. They offered a course for a few weeks with a work placement at the end of the course. As much as I did not clearly understand what I was committing myself to, I did not hesitate to enrol. At the end of the course, I got a placement in a small immigration firm working with asylum seekers. I was so happy.

At the end of the placement, I applied to volunteer at a local Citizen's Advice Bureau. At the end of two years of voluntary work, I gained a world of experience in providing advice which opened a door to apply for a permanent full-time post as an immigration adviser. I ended up working for a large immigration organisation for ten years. When the organisation closed, I went into partnership with some of my former colleagues before starting my own organisation helping migrants with their immigration needs.

One of the challenges with this role was how to progress my career. I had a dilemma between my career progression and the education and welfare of my children. One thing had to give. If I had gone for an additional course and/or a promotion, I would have become very busy and wouldn't be able to help my daughters with their education. So, I chose to stay in my comfort zone in the same position. I made sure my daughters read, did their homework and performed well in all their subjects.

Today, my biggest achievement is that my children were able to complete their university education and my eldest daughter has now completed her Master's Degree with a Distinction. Throughout the years they have shown me much love and showered me with gifts.

Living on one salary and managing the finances was a challenge. This was new to me and it was a struggle to meet the needs of the family, but we managed.

There were times when I lived on credit cards and bank loans. I was not familiar with the way utility bills were paid in the UK, so I often found myself in arrears. As my family and friends were abroad, I used to make international calls to speak with my parents, siblings and friends.

God blessed me with three strong women of God. They were living in France, Germany and Belgium. We spent hours over the phone sharing the word of God and words of encouragement. As a result, my telephone bills were £300 to £500 per month.

I remember the landlord issuing a notice of repossession of the property just a few months after my husband died. With the help of God, I found another property to rent. Viewing properties needed to be done in person back then, the children and I would get around on public transport or rely on someone else to drive us. It was tough especially in the winter months when we had to wait for the bus in the freezing cold for twenty minutes or more.

Church became my place of refuge and this is where I found both practical and spiritual support. I relied on Psalm 68: 5 "A father to the fatherless, a defender of the widows, is God in his holy dwelling." God is faithful, I witnessed His faithfulness. He has never left us nor forsaken us during all this time. He truly is who He says He is. He requires us to trust Him with all our heart, to believe He will look after us as the Good Shepherd, no matter what trials or tribulations He is right in the midst. He gives a family to the fatherless and provides a job, career, salvation and deliverance in His sovereignty. I got comfort in my daily proclamation of the word of God that says "the Lord himself goes before you and will be with you; he will never leave you nor forsake you. Do not be afraid; do not be discouraged". Deuteronomy 31:8.

While I was going through difficult times, I remembered that other people went through the same, according to 1 Peter 5:9 that says: "Resist him, standing firm in the faith because you know that the family of believers throughout the world is undergoing the same kind of suffering". I decided I would help other people in need and as I began shifting my focus onto the needs of others, God was looking after me, my home, my children, my work and my business.

I always hear this statement 'Women are resilient' sometimes it is by force of nature that you become resilient. I chose not to put my hands down but fight for my survival and that of my children. There were times I was afraid in this journey. I was afraid of not getting well-paid employment in the UK, as a woman, from an ethnic minority background with no UK experience. That fear came with worry of not being able to provide financially for my children and give them the education that their father and I wanted. There was also additional uncertainty in securing my immigration status in the UK.

When I started full-time work, my daughters were aged five and ten. Thank God my work was flexible so I was able to work either 8:00 am to 4:00 pm or 9:00 am to 5:00 pm so that I had time to get home, help with homework or attend any school meetings or activities. After dinner, I prepared the school uniform for the next day and checked school bags. Once the children had gone to bed, I would take some time to rest before going to bed, and that was only when I didn't have any church activities.

Only God knows how I managed to commute to work for three hours a day over a period of two years. And that was three hours on a good day with no heavy traffic or issues on the London Underground. I lived in East London and I worked near Heathrow Airport. My determination and motivation were to give my daughters the best life; a good education, a good career and having a relationship with their heavenly father was my drive. Saturday was the day for house cleaning and cooking. I cooked three or four different dishes to keep in the freezer for the week. After cooking, I helped my daughters with their homework before going to the local Library, or dropping them off at functions. Sunday was my big day and I always looked forward to going to church as this was where I got my comfort through prayer and hearing the word of God. I always returned home rejoicing. My children attended Sunday school, they grew up and served in the same church. I became involved in Church life as an intercessor and helped in the Sunday school ministry before being elected as a Deacon and Church Treasurer.

What helped me a lot was prayer and reading of the word of God. Almost every Sunday after church services for nearly five years, I requested prayer for various issues either with my house, work, children or being down. Every time I was prayed for, I felt better and was getting back to myself. I witnessed answered prayers and my faith grew. A few years later, I decided to help others by joining the intercessory team at my church to pray for others. Serving others helped me a lot. I have learnt in this journey called life, that as I helped others through church service or professionally, I noticed that my spirit was lifted. I began to find joy and went back to some form of normal life. Maybe that was my journey to finding myself. On the 24th April 2021, I celebrated twenty years working in Immigration Law.

What I Learned

When death strikes, it's up to us to decide whether to fight or fly. Life will throw us challenges and difficulties, but it is up to us how we decide to respond.

To you who have lost your husband or any loved ones, I say this: grief is very personal. Listen to your inner being. Take time to mourn and go through your grief but realise that your loved ones have taken their train and returned to the Creator. The one thing on Earth that is certain is death. It has no respect for age, beauty, financial position, race or profession. While waiting for your train to come, find your purpose and use the talent that God has given you. Consider your pain as an opportunity and transform it into a blessing for others. Life is very tough, let alone life without having Christ at the centre. Get to know God. When you go through tough times with Christ, he will take your burden and uplift you as you journey through the valley of weeping. Surround yourself with positive-minded people.

Keep trusting in the Lord.

Keep rejoicing in the Lord.

Keep learning new skills.

Keep hoping.

Keep loving.

Keep dreaming.

HEALING POEM

Healing arrives in all shapes and forms
Healing doesn't follow the norms
Healing differs from people to people
Healing is accustomed to the many storms

Healing does not discriminate
Healing knows no bounds
Healing is there for every case
There's enough healing to go around

Healing knows no boundaries
Healing is not proud
Healing enters in different ways
Healing enters in with no sound

Healing fights for every case
Healing has your back
Healing comes right on time
Healing covers every track

Healing will restore you to health
and healing will restore your wounds
Healing will heal your state of mind
Healing stabilises your mood

Healing gives you peace
Healing makes you smile
Healing adjusts the negatives
Healing stays for a very long while

Healing is a part of the master plan
Healing is who God is
Healing for mankind is standard
And is a part of God's will.

The Scribe

Yvonne H-Williams (Yvonne Netballer)

IG: @the_netball_scribe

AFTERWORD

At the start of the global pandemic, I had an incredible idea to continue to engage with women on the Navigating Life platform. I got together with a team from ICAN Community Church and started to share some blue sky thinking about what this could potentially mean. We shared ideas and concepts about how we could continue to engage and support women during this particular season. What started out as a 12-week program, turned into a weekly Saturday strength building, mind-stretching, empowering virtual forum, with attendees from across the world.

It was during one of these sessions that I had an idea to create an anthology, I had no idea we could even do this. The drive was to create a space for other women to share stories of how they had navigated a season in their life. I wanted for the women to be in a position to inspire other women. I'm super excited that you have read their contributions.

What next...

I hope by now you are reminded that the messenger makes the message unique and as ambassadors of hope, the women who have written these stories are sharing messages of hope, transformation, determination and sagacity.

Do you have a story of hope? Do you have a story of how you have had to navigate a season in your life? Perhaps it's time to take the first step in increasing your capacity for more and allow others to see the journey, to hear the transformation and to feel the impact of your legacy in the years to come.

NOTES

ABOUT THE AUTHORS

1. Paulette Morgan

Paulette Morgan is a Christian Life Coach specialising in Widows Coaching, Marriage Preparation Coaching, and Marriage Strengthening Coaching. She is also a Motivational Speaker to women, Author, Mentor, Wife, Mother, and Grandmother whose Purpose is helping individuals overcome limiting beliefs and fulfil their God-given potential.

Coming soon in paperback and e-book:

"Woman...Arise! Pearls of Wisdom for Woman Power."

Website: WomanArise.co.uk

Email: Paulette@WomanArise.co.uk

2. Janet McNish

Registered Counsellor, Dating & Relationship Coach, Clinical Supervisor for 24 years Janet McNish has specialized in equipping people to transform their relationships with themselves and others, through counselling, training, and broadcasting. Since 1998, Janet has effectively managed 2 Mental Health Projects, was Clinical Director for a Counselling Service and developed a team of 20 counsellors. She provides tailor-made clinical and coaching services for individuals, groups, and organizations. Janet is an engaging public speaker.

Website: www.janetmcnish.com

3. Charmaine Dawkins-Alder

I am a wife a mother sister and grandmother. I am also the business owner of Difference A Day Makes our mission passion is to make the world a safer place one day at a time through our range of Health and Safety related courses.

Email: charmaineda@hotmail.com

Facebook: Charmaine Dawkins-Alder

Instagram: @Charmaine4522

Website: www.differenceadaymakes.net

4. Faith Mathangani

I am a believer of Christ, wife and a mother of two energetic boys. Company owner & Director. Co-founder of the *More Than Us Foundation* a Non-profit organisation born out of desire to develop and empower children and families in Kenya. I live in London with my family.

Facebook: Faith Mathangani

Instagram: @faith_mathangani

Twitter: @MathanganiF

LinkedIn: Faith Mathangani

5. Doreen Douglas

Who am I? I am Doreen, a mother, a wife, a business woman, an artist and a Christian. I am a civil servant, praise & worship leader, a coach/mentor and a servant of God to minister to others. We all have a story to tell. What's yours? Greatness is in all of us. Thank you Paulette and Shania for your support.

Facebook: Doreen Douglas

Email: dorrmur10@googlemail.com

6. Simone Scott-Sawyer

Simone, formerly a legal professional, now a creative artist who writes, acts and vlogs, also works as a freelance journalist and voiceover artist. A self-confessed English grammar geek, she delights in proofreading and copy editing. She is currently chronicling her life journey's highs and lows, lifting the lid and giving a glimpse into her life to date. Connect to keep abreast with Simone's activities and purchase copies of her chronicles due out later this year.

LinkedIn:

www.linkedin.com/in/simone-scott-sawyer-664ab525

Facebook: https://www.facebook.com/simone.scottsawyer/

YouTube: https://www.youtube.com/channel/UCV05G5Vvo2QePxoFidP6dPQ/featured

7. Pauline McFarlane, Chartered FCIPD

A Business Psychologist and Founder of McFarlane & Associates Ltd, a Personal and Professional Development consultancy, working with clients to achieve their goals. Pauline's qualifications include Bsc.hons Psychology, Msc. Occupational Psychology, Postgraduate Certificate in Therapeutic Counselling and ILM coaching certification. Pauline lives in London and enjoys travelling. She is a great foodie and enjoys spending quality time with family, learning, growing and sharing, as she continues on her spiritual journey. To learn more about Pauline go to:

Website: www.mcfarlaneandassociates.com

Instagram: @lifecoach_pauline

LinkedIn: pauline-mcfarlane-1119304b

Email: mcfarlane-associates@hotmail.com

8. Precious Jason

A Multi award winning human who loves God, life, people and dark chocolate. When she is not being bossed around by a four legged creature she is desperately trying to finish her memoirs.

9. Glynis Brewster-Nathan

A retired Registered Nurse, midwife, health visitor, educator and counsellor. She has 9 biological grandchildren and over a hundred virtual grandchildren on Instagram, where she offers a caring, non-judgemental youth space to listen, discuss and offer guidance on navigating life via Instagram(@chattingwithgrandnma). She is married to Reverend Ronald Nathan of Hoggard African Methodist Episcopal Zion Church, and mother of Sherry-Ann Bobb-Toussaint and Sheldon Bobb.

Instagram: @chattingwithgranma

Email: signaturehealthplus@gmail.com

10. Shireen Morrison

Shireen and her husband are Co-founders of VisionsTvOnline, UnboundPR and UK Radio 1. They have five children and recently launched a Podcast; Young Kingz. Christian and Gospel music industry is her focus. She has a passion for new talent across genres with clients in Europe, Africa and North America.

Email:

info@visionstvonline.com

info@unboundpr.co.uk

youngkingzpodcastz@gmail.com

info@tmmpawards.com

Instagram:

@visionstvonline

@unboundpragency

@youngkingzpod

@tmmpawards

11. Anika Barnes

Anika-Adel Barnes is passionate about equality and justice for all.

Navigating Life is something that Anika endeavours to do with authenticity and strives for positive and fair outcomes for those she works with empowering them to find their own paths.

Anika has a Law degree (LLB HONS), post graduate qualification in Project in Project Management and qualifications in community justice and rehabilitation.

You will find her enjoying her two passions, being outdoors amongst the tranquillity of nature with her head immersed in a book.

12. Denise Hinkson Lawrence

A Mindset-Shifter, with a passion for transforming lives. Her signature program 'ReBirth' allows women to discover their identity, increase confidence, eliminate comparison and perfectionism for a purposeful life.

Denise is a Wife, Mother, Evangelist, Podcaster, Author and Writer, Conference Host and Speaker, Coach, and Mentor with a mandate to empower women in personal, spiritual, and leadership development. A business owner who helps women navigate difficult experiences, dismantle harmful messages about self-worth, pivot their pain to purpose, and become empowered.

"There is therapeutic value in shared stories" DHL.

Website: www.Denisehlawrence.com

Podcast: Women 2 Women **Podcast:** www.w2wpodcast.com

Instagram & Facebook: @w2wpodcast @denisehlawrencetv

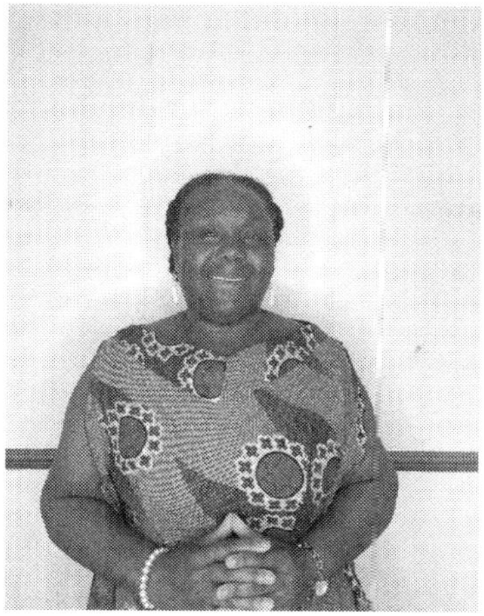

13. Jose Kalanda

Mother of two daughters. Disciple of the Lord Jesus Christ, pillar of my life working as an Immigration Advisor in the last 20 years and recently as a part time Senior Advice Worker.

Completed Master Studies in DR Congo and professional Training in the UK.

Twitter: @JoseMusau

LinkedIn: Musau Josee Kalanda

Facebook: M Josee Kalanda

Email: musaukalanda@gmail.com

ALSO BY CLAUDINE REID MBE

Navigating Life:

Health, Grief & Loss

Navigating Life:

Mindset, Identity & Relationships

ABOUT CLAUDINE REID MBE

Claudine Reid MBE

MY MISSION IS TO CREATE MORE LEADERS

Social entrepreneur, business psychologist, leadership coach, wife and mother. Claudine has more than 20 years of experience co-directing an award-winning, 7 figure social enterprise. Her expertise in growing people's talents, organisational development, and motivating others to develop successful habits make her a unique, passionate and inspirational leader and consultant.

www.claudinereidmbe.com

DIVINE FLOW PUBLISHING

Publishing People of Influence

onto Platforms for Impact.

The Lord gives the word [of power];
the women who bear and publish [the news]
are a great host. Psalm 68:11 AMPC

www.DivineFlowPublishing.com

SOME HELPFUL AGENCY NUMBERS

United Kingdom Emergency Services Number - 999

National Domestic Violence Helpline 0808 2000 247

(24-hour freephone), run by Refuge and Women's Aid.

Refuge: http://www.refuge.org.uk Supports women, children and men with services including refuges.

Women's Aid: http://www.womensaid.org.uk Working to end domestic abuse against women and children.

Samaritans: 116 123 (24 hours) http://www.samaritans.org Someone to listen, whatever people are going through.

Multiple Sclerosis - MS Society https://www.mssociety.org.uk/ Contact: 0808 800 8000

Endometriosis Society https://www.endometriosis-uk.org/ Helpline: 0808 808 2227 Telephone: 020 7222 2781

Christians Against Poverty Contact: 0800 328 0006

https://capuk.org Email: info@capuk.org

The Miscarriage Association

https://www.miscarriageassociation.org.uk/ Contact:01924 200 799 Email: info@miscarriageassociation.org.uk

Outside the UK

In the USA, the Domestic Violence Hotline is

1-800-799-SAFE (7233)

Other international helplines may be found via

http://www.befrienders.org

Printed in Great Britain
by Amazon

64826325R00121